Martin Newell is a writer, broadcaster and musician. After twenty years in rock bands, he became a pop poet in 1990. First published in *The Guardian* in 1984, he later wrote regularly for *The Independent* titles for fifteen years before taking up his current post as resident poet for *The Sunday Express* and Saturday columnist for the *East Anglian Daily Times*. In 2010 he won the *Columnist of the Year* prize at the EDF Eastern Media Awards. He has previously published a dozen collections of verse and one pop memoir: *This Little Ziggy*. He also broadcasts on Radio 4 and has presented TV programmes for BBC TV's *Inside Out* series.

Horses Seen Through Trees

Also by Martin Newell

I Hank Marvinned
Under Milk Float
The Illegible Bachelor
Poetic Licence
New! Top Poetry
This Little Ziggy*
Wildman of Wivenhoe
Black Shuck
The Song of the Waterlily
Late Autumn Sunlight
A Return To Flanders
Spoke'n'Word
Selected Poems
Prospect of Wivenhoe*

* published by Wivenbooks

Other Titles Published by Wivenbooks

Poetrywivenhoe: A Collection of New Poetry
An Essex Attitude *by Adrian May*
Invigilation *by Rex Hughes*

Horses Seen Through Trees

Snapshots of North-East Essex

MARTIN NEWELL

Wivenbooks

2010

Wivenbooks 2010
www.wivenhoebooks.com

© Martin Newell
Illustrations © Charlotte Bernays
Foreword © Andrew Phillips
Designed by Catherine Dodds

ISBN 978-0-9557313-5-8

Contents

Acknowledgements

I would like to acknowledge help,
education and inspiration from the following people.
Rev. David Thomas, John Ashdown-Hill for his inspirational
book about Mediaeval Colchester, The Victoria County History
Archive, Andrew Phillips, James Thorne, John and Shirley Bowes,
Jim Dutton, Dave Allen, Ian Callander (for telling me what a
panto isolating cock did), Mann's Music Shop, Father Alexander
Haig, Mike Bareham, Pam Dan, The Wivenhoe Bookshop, Laurie
Bussis for editing, Kate Nevard for reading and advice, Charlotte
Bernays for artwork and the many people in North-East Essex
whom I've spoken to or learned from over the years.

Remember days like these
As horses seen through trees

Foreword

I hardly know Martin Newell. I mean, I've never had a drink with him. But Martin is now a local institution: to preface his book is a privilege. He has lived the sort of raffish, romantic life that chattering critics dream of, but never achieve. He has joked, sung, and, above all, written himself into the hearts of a dour, undemonstrative, estuary Essex. He is our local Laurie Lee, an Essex Bill Bryson, and I am happy to say there are still those who think he is mad, bad and dangerous to know.

All this is evident in this book: autobiographical, nostalgic and anti-humbug; his take on North-East Essex, full of telling observations and sharp turns of phrase. It is a book you will not put down; you may even read in one sitting. So tell all your friends, pass your copy on, and encourage Mr. Newell to write another.

Andrew Phillips
historian, and author of
"Colchester: A History"

Introduction

This book is an account of the area in which I've lived and worked for over forty years. It's not meant to be a history, although, it does contain some history. Nor is it a travelogue, although I do travel a fair amount within the area. I suppose these chapters are my own stab at what is popularly called a psycho-geography, that is, an attempt to define what an area is like, how the things which have happened here have shaped it and why the people who live here are like they are.

Chiefly, the book is about North-East Essex, Colchester and some of the places which straddle the railway line to the coast. It's even not a comprehensive account. For instance, I haven't written anything about Brightlingsea, Rowhedge, St. Osyth or certain other places. This is not because I wasn't interested in them or don't like them – only because I haven't quite got around to them yet.

I've been penning a weekly article for *The East Anglian Daily Times* for over two years now. It's called *The Joy of Essex*. I've learned so much about the county while researching the articles that, combined with my own personal memories and experiences of the area, it's all added up to a fascinating picture. It's a jigsaw which I've been working on for some time now. It's nowhere near complete; but I begin, after all this time, to see what it *might* be. The more I become involved, however, the more complex it all gets, until I begin to think that the jigsaw itself might only be part of an even bigger jigsaw. In trying to examine this area in such detail, I realise that I'm also looking at a picture of England and the ever-changing English people themselves. I hope that in my own haphazard way, that I've done it justice.

Martin Newell
Wivenhoe
January 2010

Chapter 1

The Lost Country

It was only after writing *A Prospect of Wivenhoe* that I realised that it wasn't just Wivenhoe I was writing about. It was England itself – an England of small forgotten things, quiet ordinary events, and people who for the most part were not famous at all. In a world where change has accelerated almost beyond comprehension, many of us, made insecure by our own transience, try to counteract feelings of being rootless by attempting to recapture fragments of the past.

We do this in various ways. Some of us collect antiques, place carriage lamps in the drives of our estate houses, fix old wagon wheels to the gates of cottages or buy watering cans, hand-painted in the fashion of Romany barges. In the centre of Colchester there is a shop called *Past Times*. It deals in attractive, slightly twee facsimiles of the artifacts of Yesteryear. Still others of us reach a certain age and begin in semi-scholarly fashion to research our ancestry. In fact, the real past seems so elusive that a whole sub-industry has now sprung up around us, in order to sell a few broken sherds of it back to us. We buy them all eagerly: the black 1950s telephones, the pre-distressed, pre-stained patio-tables, the imitation 1920s lamps and the newly-minted compendium annuals of *Girl* or *Jackie* magazines. Such madeleines of the past are like old girlfriends and boyfriends who slipped through our fingers before we married the future. More gorgeous than ever, they just keep turning up wherever we go and they won't leave us alone.

There are 1940s dances to attend. Die-hard second-wave mods can go to scooter weekends held in former coastal holiday camps and then listen to bands that specialise in playing old Who and Small Faces songs. There are barn dances, rockabilly revivals, antique and craft fairs. Everywhere you look, the past – or some mix'n'match pre-prepped version of it – is standing seductively in a doorway, calling to you in its husky voice and pouting at you like an old whore. It's a melancholy sort of thing anyway, but for a foreigner observing, it must be redolent of watching an arthritic cat on a

sunny lawn trying, unsuccessfully, to hook down a butterfly. I know
that I myself am as afflicted with this stultifying nostalgia as anybody else. Yet I also know this much: if we gorge ourselves on the
past, we won't leave any room for the future. The Sixties, for
instance, are a good case in point.

Of all the decades of the past century, the Sixties is the one that
we seem to get most misty-eyed about. It's also the one that we revisit most frequently and reinterpret worst. Put a poster up practically
anywhere in the kingdom with the words *Sixties Nite* on it and watch
them go. You won't be able to move for terrible trousers, kaftans,
day-glo paisley dresses and regulation issue hippie wigs. The entire
decade – which in reality, was a jump-cut sequence of several quite
distinct mini-eras – will then be reduced to a few silk scarves, forty
worn out tunes and a packet of joss sticks. The pathos of this occasionally makes me feel like nutting a wall in despair.

Who remembers the pre-Beatles pop charts, replete with Joe
Brown, Joe Meek, Del Shannon and The Shadows? They were the
Sixties too. What about the jazz – Stan Getz, Blossom Dearie or
Miles Davis? Who recalls the sheepskin car coats advertised in the
Exchange & Mart or those peculiar string fabric beige-coloured driv-
ing-gloves? What about Trilby hats with a little feather in the brim?
Nice glass of Creamola Foam or Mateus Rose, anyone? And how
about all those equally good, yet half-forgotten chart singles: the
soaring brilliance of The Hollies' *I Can't Let Go*, The Yardbirds'
Heartful of Soul or Spencer Davis's *Time Seller*?

My own most-prized bit of clothing in 1962, aged nine, was
actually my snake-buckle elasticated belt, bought for about two bob
from Woolworths. How quickly times changed. Only six years later,
aged fifteen, it was a Hendrix-style military jacket with a red collar,
yellow epaulettes and frogged sleeves. It didn't win me any points.
In fact, it got me pointed at and eventually beaten-up in the street.
I'd have been safer with a windcheater and some ice-blue drainies.
In the Sixties the food was ghastly, the wine was undrinkable and
most people looked short haired and rather ordinary. In 1967 too,
unbelievably, Engelbert Humperdinck managed to keep The
Beatles' *Penny Lane* off the top-spot for about six weeks. Oh, and
country buses still ran, the trains were filthy but fairly regular and
Mr. Wilson, the PM, went to the Scilly Isles for his holidays.

Though it was all rather *smashing* because, in retrospect, the Sixties seemed sunny and cheerful. They were a bit like the Fifties – only in colour and with extra pocket money. But hardly anybody, apart from a few rich young things in London, ever launched into a freak-dance in the middle of Hyde Park. Most of us didn't even think of the time as "The Sixties". And even then we never twigged that it was all over until about 1977 when the next fashionistas, along with Mrs. Thatcher, started saying how harmful it had been.

And yet, when it was all going on, you knew that something was afoot – the minute that Cliff and the Shads got on that double-decker bus in *Summer Holiday* (1962). Just like you knew that Holly Golightly was onto something special in *Breakfast At Tiffany's* (also 1962). That was when the Sixties really started. It was a whiff of freedom and optimism – even for the pinstriped clerks and the houndstooth-checked secretaries eating their sandwiches in London parks. It was a notion that practically anything might happen next. The Sixties were also good because the milkmen still whistled. In fact, there were still milkmen. The Sixties were one sunny day in the rainy week that was the 20th century.

This is why, one day recently, I couldn't stay away from an exhibition at the Colchester Castle Museum. For there, in an upstairs gallery, was *The Sixties Seen*, a lovingly put together display of the fabrics, the fashions, the artwork and some of the iconography of that much-hyped, vanished decade. In one piece, glass framed, were ten essential pop albums, six of which I'd owned at one time or another. One in particular, *The Who Sell Out* (1967) was the first album I'd ever bought. It had cost me a month's worth of my paper-round money. I loved it so much that I played it before I went to school each morning.

Among my fellow guests at the Castle Museum exhibition's first view – many themselves now in their fifties and sixties – one or two sported creditable attempts at Sixties costume. There were also quite a few *Sixties Nite* style disasters. It was a little melancholy at times, but then these clothes *were* originally meant to be worn by skinny youngsters. Our guest speaker was Carolann Jackson, former production-assistant on *Ready Steady Go*, the most revered pop programme of the decade. Carolann gave a short but uplifting speech about her time on the show. She'd met absolutely everybody, of course – even the Rolling Stones and George Harrison. And she'd witnessed Jimi Hendrix's first British gig at the Scotch of St. James Club. She disputed the cliché that if you remembered the Sixties, you weren't there. For she had been there – right at the heart of it – and did remember. For a small exhibition, *The Sixties Seen* was highly comprehensive. Nostalgic it may be, but it also reminds you that, above all else, those Sixties pioneers were futurists. They weren't looking back. Mostly, they were looking forward. That's the bit that no one nowadays seems to remember.

As many of our growing band of amateur genealogists discover, despite our best hopes, most of us *aren't* descendants of royalty who should today rightfully be king. Most of us *aren't* aristocracy who were only deprived of their true status because – according only to family hearsay – an ancestor was born out of wedlock. The Great House up the road, which might have been ours had history not so unfairly taken against us, *isn't* the inheritance which fate has cheated us out of. Most of us *aren't* descended from Eleanor of Aquitaine, Lord Nelson or Cleopatra. And even if we *were* – so what? The truth is that the majority of us are descended from farm-labourers, weavers, soldiers, servants, seamstresses and husband-men. If we really want to find out who we are, we would do as well to talk to our older relatives before they die off – even to read the diaries and accounts of strangers – rather than to trail around haplessly looking at old church records, in the forlorn hope of discovering a dalliance between a below-stairs serving girl and a duke.

I wanted to write about the provincial English people. I do this not out of any sense of nationalism, but out of sheer curiosity. I wanted to find out where I sprang from. I reasoned that I was just as likely to find a few more missing pieces of this battered old jigsaw by talking to others, as I was by traipsing across a worthy but arid desert of written historical and genealogical record. I wanted to try and write about all the little things that the historians and documentary-makers miss out. I wanted to scavenge, maybe, like a dog might after a banquet. What I'm finding is that the further I go in, the vaster it all gets. And yet, conversely, the more I find that – as a friend of mine says – "Everything is joined up with a bit of string." But first, I thought I should quickly glance at what I knew about my own family.

> *Here's a jack – a jack for thee*
> *And here's another, good as he*

Here's a third – the best of the three
And there's old Jack-in-the-apple tree

The above rhyme was taught to me, as a child, by my late father. It was recited in an old country card game called *Jack-in-the-Apple Tree* and was taught in turn to him, when he was a boy, by an old thresher. In between the wars his father, a professional soldier and Great War veteran, kept a pub called *The Duke of Wellington* in a Kent village called Ryarsh. The village had a population of only a few hundred people. It was during the poverty-hobbled 1930s and times were far from easy. Three or four children used to die of diphtheria each winter, he told me. If a child was born with something wrong with it – Down's Syndrome for instance – sometimes, he said, the midwife would quietly turn the infant on its face, stifling it at birth. If this seems brutal in modern-day terms, you must first begin to try and understand how poor many people were.

There was very little money about. His father, Charlie, might find a brace of peasants hanging in the porch one morning – left by a hard-up farm worker in lieu of payment, in order to settle a beer tally. In these hard times a local farmer would occasionally take his own life with a shotgun, as a result of insoluble debt. Charlie, who had been a medic in the trenches of Flanders during the Great War and who, as a result, had a strong stomach for such things, would receive a knock on the door in the small hours: "Charlie?" the village policeman would enquire: "We've got a bit of a mucky one. Can you give us a hand?" Charlie would go. In September, the hop-pickers came down from London, many of them poor families who treated the work as a holiday away from the grime of the city. Some of the hop-pickers could be rather rough. If a fight broke out in the bar, Charlie would be over the counter laying about them with a poker. "I've got your money – now piss off!" he bawled at closing time. "People thought it was tremendously funny," my dad remembered, "but he meant it."

Before the Second World War broke out, my dad and his brother, still only boys, took work on local farms at a shilling a day. "One boy is half the work. Two boys is a quarter o' the work. And three boys is no work at all!" the farmer told them. If the local copper caught the boys stealing birds' eggs, they'd hide them under their caps. But he was too fast. He'd pat them on the head roughly, giving them a rub for good measure and say: "*There's* good lads." Then he'd send them on their way with the smashed eggs all over their hair. If they scrumped apples, the orchard owner, if he caught them at it, blazed away with a shotgun, its cartridges filled with rice shot, which peppered their legs painfully but didn't injure them.

When I later interviewed my father for some research I was doing on the subject of gardening during the interwar years, other interesting stuff emerged about country life. By contrast with today, nothing was ever wasted. The family lavatory was 'an earth closet'. It consisted of a slit trench, which was dug a spit narrow, three feet long and three feet deep. The buckets: "two wet and one sloppy" from the pub's outside toilet were emptied into this trench and covered with earth. When the trench was about a third full, it was filled in and a new one was dug. When that particular corner of the pub's kitchen garden was done with, it was cordoned off, left for a year and then planted with vegetables the following year. A new portion of ground was now designated for the job of earth closet. And so it went on.

In 1938, aged eleven, my father caught polio – a not uncommon thing in those days. In the early days of the war, still wearing a calliper on his leg, with his father and brother enlisted and posted far away, it fell to him – on Ministry of Agriculture orders – to dig up the pub's large lawn for the growing of food. He told me that he occasionally got a bit of advice or help from a sympathetic passing villager. Mainly, though, he had to struggle with it all himself, since his mother was now having to run the village pub all on her own:

"Green beans, we salted and stored in jars," he said. "Potatoes, we clamped. That is, we stored them in a square pit for winter – layer of straw, layer of spuds, layer of straw, layer of spuds, etc. Onions, if they'd been good sets, you kept the seed back. You tied a muslin bag 'round the flower head to catch the seeds, so you could use them the next year. Tomatoes, you went down to see the man at the local sewage plant for. The best and strongest seedlings grew there and you gave the man sixpence and came back with a box of them to plant out." Every so often, a man from nearby Maidstone came round to clean the village streets in Ryarsh. His name was Mr. Unwin and he had a small cart drawn by a donkey, with M.U.D.C.– the initials of Maidstone Urban District Council – painted on it. "For years," my dad laughed, "When I was a boy, I thought the letters stood for Mr. Unwin's Donkey Cart."

When I was seventeen, I took a job out at Ardleigh on a pig farm. "Pigs?" my dad had asked me: "Good fun. I always liked pigs." He'd had some experience of them himself, both as a boy and then many years later, after military service, when he'd visited farms as an environmental health officer. During the last Foot and Mouth crisis, he despaired of both the government and the modern ignorance of rural affairs alike. He'd been involved in an earlier outbreak of the disease, during the 1960s. "People these days," he said, "think that farmers are these ruthless people trying to profit from us all. They were actually very fond of the beasts in their charge," he explained. He told of a northern farmer whom he sometimes drank with, wandering disconsolately 'round an empty barn the night after his beasts had been compulsorily slaughtered. Out of habit, the first night, the farmer had taken his lantern out to the shed to check up on his cattle, which he'd forgotten were now no longer there. And my dad shook his head, tutted and shrugged.

The Newells, before my dad was born, if they weren't serving in the army, were grooms and ostlers from Brandon way in Suffolk. They married the Wards from Kent, who were farming folk. The Wrights on my mum's dad's side were farm labourers from Necton, near Swaffham in Norfolk. The Cranfields on my mum's mother's side kept an ironmonger's shop in Islington. I have a picture of them standing in cloth caps, hobnailed boots and Victorian pinnies on a city allotment which was crammed with cabbages. The family all gardened. Many of them knew about horses – working horses, that is. Some were carriage men and dray-drivers. My dad's brother, Tony, later married a bluff, cheerful country girl, called June, from Buckinghamshire and they kept a smallholding there. Here my older cousins grew up in the 1960s, shooting air rifles at rats in barns and living in their wellies.

When I talk to the some of the older inhabitants of north Essex, the stories they tell me are immediately recognizable, because they are more or less the same ones that my family told me. Even their faces are similar. They *way* they talk – apart from a slight difference in accent – is similar. There is the same modesty, the same reluctance to over-dramatise, the same politeness, and the same self-deprecating humour. They are the people of the Lost Country. They are the English.

Chapter 2

Is My Team Ploughing?

Essex is about seventy percent rural – a fact that I never tire of cudgelling people with. Despite the endless springing up of new housing "in sympathetic local style" there's still a fair amount of the old county left. We're a funny lot in this country. Many of us are in a sort of Decree Nisi situation with our souls and the nearest we get to spiritual is that vague concept which we call 'the countryside'. We like to think that it's being looked after. We do odd things in order to stay in touch with it. We watch programmes on TV which involve border collies rounding up sheep. We attend country fairs and get tearful over old tractors. Indeed, some of us even stand in rude shelters with total strangers all weekend, staring at small birds through binoculars. Many of us feel more inclined to buy a pot of chutney or a bottle of beer if it has a picture of a ploughman on it – or a checked gingham lid sewn by somebody called Mrs. Bridges. In a spiritually skint age, we like to ask: "Is my team still ploughing?" and to hope fervently that it still is. The closest many of us get to the country, though, is a walk or cycle along a prescribed route marked by posts with little arrows on them.

Tendring district is full of working farms. Despite this fact, nowadays the majority of us hardly ever meet farmers. It can be an illuminating thing when we do. About a five-minute walk up the road from my own house in Wivenhoe is Ballast Quay farm, run by John Bowes. John, now in his early seventies, with 125 acres of land and 120 cattle, was born at the farm. His father took the place on in 1928 and was a dairy farmer. John's eldest brother delivered the town's milk until 1962. In 1972, John went over from dairy farming to beef, which is sold at Colchester Market. John's cattle were spared the horror of the last Foot and Mouth crisis, although, at one point the disease came within only a few miles of the place. Back then, no one saw John for weeks. People asked after him daily in the local where he played darts. He couldn't bring himself to watch TV during this time. "It used to upset me," he said quietly.

It's true that it was a grim and depressing time. For the New Labour government, the honeymoon period was very much over. With the raw wheals of the Kosovo war and the Fuel Protests barely healed on its flanks, it now fell headlong into an unexpected major domestic crisis. This was the first-ever British government with a cabinet whose members, for the most part, had absolutely no direct experience of rural matters. Here were no gentleman farmers or old Patricians. Never mind beer and sandwiches, these guys were strictly café latté, sun-dried tomatoes and polenta. When the Foot and Mouth Crisis arrived in February of 2001, they freaked. The hapless Minister for Agriculture, Nick Brown, was by all accounts a perfectly nice man. But he was one who was entirely ill-equipped to deal with the emerging crisis. For him, it would turn out to be a baptism of fire – literally. A former Chief Whip, outed as gay by the *News of The World* a couple of years earlier, he had no ostensible background in farming and did not inspire confidence in the dismayed and pessimistic farming community.

The epidemic, which rapidly raged its way across the sodden countryside, was a mystery and the media flailed frantically around looking for someone to point the finger at. Yet, what *was* Foot and Mouth Disease and how did it spread? Answers were unsatisfactory. It was a cold weather plague, we were told – possibly carried on the back of the sleety wind. It was a pestilence of biblical magnitude, which caused widespread, almost superstitious, panic. The remedies and edicts which were used to combat it were correspondingly medieval. "Burn all the beasts!" boomed the witch-hunters. Compassionate Middle England threw up its hands in horror. Burn them? But where? The distressing televisual footage of thousands of beasts being immolated on filthy pyres throughout the length and breadth of the land went around the world. This was a holocaust. Now the authorities closed the footpaths down. Wivenhoe woods were out-of-bounds, the towpath along the River Colne was closed, and glum dogwalkers were to be seen trudging the rainy lanes with pockets full of plastic bags, because there was nowhere now to walk the dog. Unimaginably, the English countryside was closed down overnight and pronounced out-of-bounds. It was soul corroding and profoundly depressing. The government had demonstrated very clearly that they really *had* lost touch with the very land that bore them.

One cold sunny morning in early spring of 2008, I sat in their
house with John Bowes and Shirley, his wife of fifty years. John was
born in 1936 in the very room where we sat. In the eight years
before he was born, he said, two owners had run the place but then
had quickly gone broke. "Attenborough was one name. They grew
fruit and sprouts, that sort of stuff. There were sprouts sat behind
the house there, and there were blackcurrants behind the wood."
John described farming as a happy, if not particularly remunerative
life: "The first twenty-two years was very hard. We did it the old way
– our father's way – 'cos he knew nothing different. He believed in
the binder and the thrashing drum coming in... all the dust." He
coughed heartily and then added: "But I think modern farming is
brilliant."

On one side of John Bowes' family, like my own, his grandfather had been an army man who ended up running a pub – the
long-closed Anglesea Arms in Queens Road. "In those days, people
took a pub just to keep a roof over their head." said John. He can't
remember that much about his forbear – apart from the fact that
he'd originally come from Hereford and had been discharged from
service because of ill health. The other side of the family however
had come from just over the border in Hertfordshire and John also
had two uncles who farmed at Fordham and Aldham.

Ballast Quay Farm, as you walk up Anglesea Road onto the
farm track, lies to the right. The 1830s brick cowsheds and the
muddy yard with its outbuildings echo to the sound of cattle, chickens and geese. It's a proper old-fashioned working English farm
with bits of old farm machinery lying about, poultry going about its
business and a dog barking somewhere in the middle distance.
People wander in and out of the yard all the time. Here, in a shed
which John lent him, Max Tannahill, the artist gets on with his
work, carving pieces of driftwood into the shapes of fish and birds
for his exhibitions. John has a certain amount of time for artists,
having been a member of the old Wivenhoe Arts Club. More often
than not, John's grandson Jamie will be working nearby, up a ladder
in overalls doing some welding on a steel boat. "He's a clever boy."
Shirley says proudly.

Elsewhere around the yard during the day, along with the stan-
dard sonic backdrop of chickens and cattle, are the sounds of hammering, sawing or machinery. Now David, one of John's sons, will

round the corner into the yard, bring his tractor grumbling and stuttering to a halt by the shed and then get down and walk into the house for tea. This, I have said, is a proper, working farm. It's also very much a family concern, with sons, daughters, grandchildren and friends, coming, going and lending a hand as and when required.

In one of the other brick sheds, there's a door marked with a painted cross. Billy the Fish, the fisherman-turned-farmhand, stayed here for a while when he was helping around the farm. One afternoon, in early autumn of 1994, both of us having finished work for the day, Billy and I sat in the yard drinking cider from plastic bottles and having a bit of a yarn. Squadrons of midges wheeled in formation in the balmy air, then John Bowes came by, driving a few cattle in front of him, and stopped for a chat. The sun, lower in the sky as the season turned on its axis, came through the trees and settled onto the red brick walls behind us in dappled patches. A gentle breeze came winnowing up from the south. It was, for that brief moment, perfect. I was due to fly to Japan the following day and I recall thinking: "If the plane crashes, or for some reason I don't get back, I want to remember this."

A straightforward sort of man with an occasional mild stutter, when he wishes to emphasize a point, John Bowes has the memory of an elephant and can tell great stories. Billy used to reckon that the best time to catch him was in the feed-shed during the morning. Here, you would get an unrivalled mixture of country wisdom and unprintable views about recent governments, which Billy was by turns amused by and in awe of. Once, when Billy saw me working with a pitchfork, jungle-bashing a garden in the village, he asked me where I'd found it. "Thorpe Market – before it closed." I told him. "I've got a spare too."

Billy asked that since it was Farmer John's sixtieth birthday approaching, could he have one of the pitchforks off me for a present? I said of course he could – but didn't John have enough pitchforks? Billy replied that the old-style pitchforks were hard to come by these days. I handed it over. "How you gonna wrap it?" I shouted after him. "Carefully, Mart'n, f***in' carefully!" he yelled back, as he disappeared down Alma Street on the battered old bicycle which he called "The Comp'ny Vehicle". Shortly afterwards, Lizzie, one of John's daughters, brought me a book and asked me if I would sign it for him. I wiped my hands, took the pen and wrote, "Happy Birthday John – You've been like a farmer to me."

Since he left school in 1951, John Bowes has never known anything but farming. In a modern world whose main themes are transience and change, the sheer steady permanence of life at Ballast Quay Farm is hard to illustrate, except in small vignettes – like so many snapshots tipped out from an envelope onto a table and which you might randomly leaf through. John's wife, Shirley, was born in Hamilton Road, Wivenhoe. Her mother was one of thirteen girls, most of whom had gone into service. Her father was in Air Sea Rescue and used to help John's father out with the harvest when he was needed. John and Shirley first met when both of them were very young children. They courted in nearby bluebell woods and Billy once told me that to this day John still brings Shirley the first batch of bluebells into the house each spring.

In answer to a question about holidays, John said: "We got married in 1957. We didn't have a holiday till 1968 and we went to Gorleston, where we stayed in a caravan. We had a wonderful holiday there. My father died on the 1st January '68. We had our first holiday with six children and Shirley's parents. They had a caravan and some of the kids stayed with them. Then in the 1970s with Pat Green and Maurice we used to go to Corton, just the other side of Lowestoft. We went to Warners Holiday camp at Corton for 8 years, just before it burnt down."

"We haven't got passports." Shirley added: "We've got passport *forms*, partly filled in. That's as far as we've got – so far"

Gazing out across John's fields, the Colne Valley is spread out before you. You can look out at the silver hazy estuary, at the distant white yachts, the gravel boats on the choppy River Colne, the endless farmland and the bird-loud saltings at low tide. In the foreground are copses, woods and the marshes, where John's cattle graze in high summer. The Clacton trains rumble across Ballast Quay Farm and just down the slope from the farm buildings are a couple of overgrown brick arches and the remains of an untended orchard, which in autumn is still laden with apples. Billy and I always swore that if we could borrow Osea Island's cider press – which I'd managed to do a few years earlier – we'd get some cider made out of them. John complains that he's a bit overrun with foxes at the moment, which have depleted the poultry somewhat. "We shoot them if we see them but we haven't got much poultry left. The foxes go into the dairy in the farm buildings and take the broody hens off the eggs." There are other visitors too, including the muntjac deer which appear, leaving their footprints in the mud in wet weather and the mallards, which sometimes nest in the largely unused front porch of the house. John's main business though, is with his cattle.

"We used to walk the store cattle every year to the marshes at Wivenhoe Station. We used to walk them down the village. We used to get enough people up for the job, so some went ahead to block the roads off. That's before Dene Park was built. We'd turn the cattle down Queens Road, stop them going up Park Road, stop them going up the High Street, turn them down at Perce Chaney's shop, stop them running down Clifton Terrace, stop them going to the church, down Station Road and then through the toll-gate onto the marshes. Only once do I remember them coming back by lorry. It was when the marshes flooded. We lived at River View then and I can't tell you the year. We lived there for thirty two and a half years. The noise of cattle walking through water is...ooh, a strange noise. They were right up at the far corner. Used to be beautiful elm trees at the far corner of those marshes. They were wonderful trees."

Shirley said: "We had beautiful ones all along this meadow in the Sixties, before the Dutch Elm Disease came." John added: "That opened the country up when Elm Disease came. I'd rather have the elm trees. The elm trees we had here – we had a kestrel build in one here. We had owls. Mallards built in them. Jackdaws built in them. I've got oak stumps in that bit of green down the bottom. The one that since fell over – there were barn owls in that, jackdaws and mallard ducks. Bats used to come out of the elm trees."

I did hear once that John wasn't too fond of horses. When I asked him about the old ploughing days, though, he said: "My father had a horseman, Jim Thompson, from Alresford. He was a Scotsman. We had two horses – Duke and Prince. When Jim Thompson left us to go to Harold Dutton, Father sold Harold Dutton the horses as well. We went into tractors then, after the war. But they were still using horses and plough during and after the war..." And here we paused, since I felt that I'd taken up quite enough of John's morning.

The insight which I got from talking to John on his home-ground was perhaps subtly different to that which I'd gleaned from various yarning sessions I'd had with him in the pub over the years. It was like seeing a film on the big screen, with full surround-sound, having previously, only watched it on a small monochrome TV. When, once again, I consider that Essex is still seventy percent rural, it's surprising how invisible this rurality is. It seems not only to be invisible to our rulers in Westminster, but also to many of the people who may only live within half a mile of it. Unfortunately, where there *is* an interest in the countryside, it often comes from those serious-minded souls who march determinedly along the foot-ways, talking about the environment and militantly protecting various endangered species. In this quarter, there is often to be found a suspicion of farmers. Farmers are seen, sometimes, as rather uncaring, exploitative people who need to be re-educated about the very land that bore them. The truth is that most of our farmers in modern media-savvy Britain, don't really have a voice. By the very virtue of what they do and where they live, they don't have the time to go out doing lecture tours, writing books or appearing on the *Jonathan Ross Show*. One day, as we did during two world wars, we may come to depend on them again. With any luck, it won't be because of an emergency such as war. It may instead be that the much desired self-sufficiency which certain classes constantly chunter on about will begin to become a reality. Our farmers already know their job. It is *we* who need re-educating.

Chapter 3

Over To Sunny Arm

As I began this chapter, I stopped to make a cup of tea and I turned the radio on. There, on the Nation's Favourite Station, a woman, whom with the best will in the world, I can only call a bloody stupid dollop, was busy telephoning the mid-morning phone-in programme to complain about farm animals being treated cruelly. There were, she said, lambs and calves being left out in the fields in wind, rain and sleet. And shouldn't there be some sort of legislation to make farmers provide shelter for them? At first I thought it was a joke. It wasn't. She was being perfectly serious. She went on to say that the RSPCA were also concerned about the matter and that there ought to be a campaign. To answer her query, the BBC fielded a farmer from the Brecon Beacons – another woman, as it happened. She was very measured and patient in her reply, explaining that the sheep all had nice woolly jackets and the cattle, stout leather ones. She pressed home further the point that animals had lived in inhospitable conditions long before man began farming them. The first woman was undeterred. Fifteen percent of the younger animals died of exposure, she said, and how did we know that animals didn't feel the cold? Furthermore, they should be given shelters – after all, horses in bad weather were given high-tog outdoor covers. Shouldn't we be doing the same for the lambs, many of which were out in daytime temperatures as low as ten degrees? This, in one simple paragraph, is the sort of modern ignorance embedded in the minds of certain sections of the public. And this is what our hapless farmers are currently faced with.

About a quarter of a mile along John Bowes' track, across the Alresford Road, is Sunnymead Farm.

During the early '80s, I used to go up there with a barrow once a week, to get a bale of straw for the poultry, which I used to keep then. The arrangement was that you left fifty pence in the front porch and just went and hoiked yourself down a bale from the dry side of the barn. In those days, some of the letters on the farm's sign had fallen off, so that what you read as you arrived there, was the name 'Sunny arm'. This is what my young stepdaughter used to call the place, anyway.

The farmer at Sunnymead Farm is Jim Dutton, a Quaker, and a man whom John Bowes calls, 'an excellent chap'. Jim's dad, Harold, with no previous experience of farming, took the place on in 1930 and made a good job of it. Like John, Jim – a couple of years younger – was born in the farmhouse where he now still resides. I cycled over to see him one wet evening in late winter. The room in which we sat seemed terribly familiar to me and reminded me of a room in my late uncle's farmhouse. There, along one wall, was the same type of heavy, brown, varnished sideboard, which many of us grew up with. Here also, was a large oval table with a tablecloth on it. A dog was barking in another room somewhere and I could hear someone shushing it. Jim's 1949 ledger book was on the table, a reference to which crops the farm had grown, who had worked there and what they'd been paid. Unlike John, Jim, a softly spoken, almost donnish man, went to Cambridge University where he did a science tripos before eventually returning to agriculture. Mostly a seed farmer now, he still grows a bit of barley every year, which he sells to John Bowes. His son David also works and lives on the farm. The Duttons originally came from Chester in the north-west of England. Jim's mother had been a doctor in Manchester. Like the Bowes, Jim and his wife, Gwyneth, go back a long way. Gwyneth was a teacher and first met Jim at the Friends School when the two of them were children. They met again later as adults, when Gwyneth was teaching there and Jim was asked to invigilate at the school examinations. They've been together ever since.

In earlier years and up until 1977, Sunnymead Farm had kept pigs. In an echo of my own father's words, Jim said: "My father liked pigs." It's a thing that people these days might find surprising, but many people in the area, during the war and for years afterwards kept pigs. Many domestic households with a garden, or even a bit of a yard, kept a pig. John Bowes had confirmed this fact to me earlier. He'd said: "I left school in 1951 and even then, you could make five pounds profit on a pig when a lot of men's wages were only two pounds a week. I mean, behind Wivenhoe Station, what they called the Shunting Shed, was all pigsties. We had six sows and a boar. We've still got the pig-book where Father would let the boar out or people would bring sows *to* the boar."

Jim Dutton, though, got out of pig farming when the bottom dropped out of the market and is glad he did so, remarking that in earlier days, regulations for keeping pigs were nowhere near as stringent as they are now. "Rules and regulations again" he says ruefully. He remembers, many years ago, reclaiming the marshland in what he calls 'the valley' of his farm. Irish labourers dug it out by hand, drained it and then dragged or blasted the tree-stumps out. The old village doctor, William Dean, got them the gelignite to do the job. In pre- Health and Safety days, William brought it back by train in a heavy case. "The train guard, helping him to lift it out, asked him, 'What have you got in there then William – a bomb?' " Jim laughs. "I bet you didn't know that one."

Doctor Dean was the family GP when Jim was a child and was also present at the birth of John Bowes. It is mind-boggling in our safety-obsessed times, that if there was ever an occasion where you might have felt the need to use a case of gelignite, you simply got your family GP to go and fetch it for you on the train. Try running that one past Health and Safety now, or, come to think of it, the reception team at the Wivenhoe Medical Centre.

At a hundred and seventy-six acres, Sunnymead Farm – like Ballast Quay, is another traditional English farm with its woodland, fields and old brick buildings. I've cycled across it in all seasons now, for the best part of three decades, passing the rye, the kale and the occasional blue haze of linseed flowers. I have a strange story to relate here. For years, in a dip along the track before I approached Cockayne's Wood, I'd see a large flat field to the left of the brook. I used to have an almost psychic feeling at times that it ought to have been a lake. One day, a friend working at Ordnance Survey sent me an 1895 map of Wivenhoe and there it was – my ghost lake. Its old name had been Villa Pond, although it had been drained many years before and then turned into growing land. At the turn of the millennium, however, Jim turned the strange flat field back into a lake again, thereby exorcising the odd feeling that I'd always had about it.

The turn of the millennium also brought a strange drama to Sunnymead Farm. Jim Dutton, with his scientific background had agreed to grow a GM maize crop on his land. He had no idea at the time that it would lead to the subsequent tumult, which it eventually did. The first I heard about the matter was one weekday evening in The Greyhound pub. A group of people came into the place mid-evening, obviously very fired-up about something. "I'd have thought *you* would have been at tonight's meeting, Martin?" said one of them, semi-accusingly. I told him that I hated meetings of any sort but, anyway, what was it all about?

"This GM crop that they're going to grow in Wivenhoe." I was told. And now I was filled in with the details. Everyone had the zeal of the righteous in his eyes. It would be the end of the world, they said. It was dangerous. It was evil. Something should be done, etc, etc. I was a writer; didn't I have a duty to say something about it all? And what did I think of GM food? I said that I never ate anything else. I pointed out that my old border collie was a genetically-modified dog of a sort. I added that if there was anyone there who smoked skunkweed, then they were almost certainly smoking genetically-modified dope and so, therefore, what was the problem with eating the food? This was not taken as a joke. Once again I was informed in no uncertain terms that *they* were poisoning the land. "*They* are our farmers, for Christsakes. They grow our food." I replied.

In the post-meeting heat of the evening, this remark went down like bad flatulence in a lift and I was told it was obvious whose side *I* was on. I reasoned that even if *they* did want to experiment, wasn't it better that *they* did it under the public gaze, rather than conduct things secretly, perhaps in the un-monitored vastness of some private estate? This cut no ice with the protesters either. A group with a clunkily acronymic name: *Concerned Residents Of Wivenhoe* (CROW) was formed. More meetings were held, statements were issued and once again, it was pledged that something would be done.

Something was done, though not by the members of CROW. A short while later, a group of outsiders came in one evening and tore up the crop in one of Jim Dutton's fields. Only after the protesters were arrested did it transpire that they'd torn up the *wrong* maize crop in the wrong field. Poor old Jim, more bemused and disappointed than angry about the invasion, said that the protesters had assumed the GM crop was in the field *without* any weeds growing amongst it. The whole point of the experiment, he said, was to ascertain possible environmental damage. The weeds, therefore, grew freely among the GM maize plants but had been eradicated among the natural maize. The protesters, when the case came to court, eventually got themselves acquitted, leaving the baffled farmer and his son to clear up in their wake. The GM experimenters themselves, presumably, went off and conducted their research a little more quietly elsewhere. In a nasty little twist in this tale, Jim later discovered that persons unknown, had poisoned all the fish in his lake. Well, *that* went well, didn't it? Hooray for free protest and all its adherents who are helping to keep our ruthless farmers on message

As I asked in the last chapter: Is our team still ploughing? Just about, it is, yes. John Bowes, Jim Dutton and their boys have survived war, pestilence and the myriad edicts of successive governments who have tinkered and dibbled for decades with their lives and work. Though, most of us, who know next to nothing about the subject – other than what we read in the more engaged national broadsheets – will continue to twitter on about organic produce, pesticides and animal rights, preferring to place our faith in Mrs. Bridges and her gingham lids, rather than in farmers John and Jim. This, as we might say round here, is a bit of a rum old do.

Chapter 4

Bloody Newcomers

There's a saying that he who teaches, learns twice. I recently helped out with some classes for German teenagers at a summer school. They needed an articulate and sober person with local knowledge to help them improve their spoken English. They got me instead. I decided to arrange the chairs in the room as if they were train seats and took the students on a virtual journey from Colchester to Clacton. I explained to them that the language that they were now learning, a fair amount of it anyway, including many place names, had originated in Lower Saxony, in Germany. We left from Colchester Town. Hythe, our first stop, I said was an old English word for a harbour – like their word *hafen*. Wifa was thought to be the Saxon who gave his name to Wivenhoe. Aegel was the Saxon who gave his name to Alresford. The word 'ford' is itself derived from the West Germanic, *furdu*, like the 'furt' in Frankfurt. Thorrington was once *Torenduna*, a settlement among thorns, whilst Clacc, another Saxon, gave his name to Clacton. The name-origins of Thorpe-le-Soken, where rail passengers change for Kirby, Frinton and Walton, are rather more complex. The 'Thorpe' part is Norse, the 'le' is Norman and the 'Soken' or *soke* was a Saxon word for an area of land. Many of our other words, like 'bring', 'send', 'ring' and 'stink' are still pretty much the same in modern German too.

I asked the students, in turn, to pretend that they were the station announcer and to read out the unfamiliar names on the blackboard. I read them out in BBC English. Now I read them out in a local accent. I wanted them to know what the old north Essex accent sounded like. I told them that in our relatively small country, we had an unusual diversity of accents and that as they travelled around the place, they would discover this.

As I will mention in my yet-to-be-written history of Essex grammar: *The Way We Was*, it's pretty rare nowadays to hear anyone under fifty using the old Essex accent. The conventional wisdom on the subject is that we've all been drowned in the tsunami of Estuarine English now spoken by Wyne, Jawdan, Tiffny and Danyella. Milk has become 'miwk'. An Indian meal has become 'a

ninja miw' and a statement has become a question? Mockney has
fused with Jafaican. Glottal stops and blurred consonants have
hitched a ride on the cadences of American and Australian tea-time
soaps. The old dialect of the East Saxons is now deeper underwa-
ter than Old Dunwich

Thirty or so years ago, a few of us in our waggish twenties
thought it was funny to stand around talking in the accents of the
'good owld buoys' whom we'd worked alongside or heard in pubs:

"How ever *aare* yew?" one of us would ask another. "Not
s'baad. Yeew?" you'd respond. It became such a habit that years
later, whenever any of us bump into each other, we'll still lapse
straight back into it again. Underneath all the good-natured mick-
ey-taking though, was a genuine affection for the accents which our
grandfathers had used. For instance, you never said "one or two" if
you could say, "A couple or three." You never said, "Goodbye."
Instead you said, "Yeahp. Seeyagin." or "Moindow yergoo!" Old
women remarked to their grandchildren, "Well, hevven't you
growen?" and there, hidden in that last verb are the final shreds of
Middle English, in its turn directly descended from the Old High
German, "gruoan." Another interesting thing is that in places, the
Essex accent, in both cadence and tone often sounds Australian. It's
not easy to imitate, either. Even people who've lived in this area for
decades, when trying to mimic old Essex, will fall into Mummerset,
that risible all-purpose rural accent formulated by the BBC for use
in their everyday tales of country folk.

Welcome then, to Essex, ancient kingdom of the East Saxons.
It was they, who gave their name to the seax, that scimitar-like
sword, three of which adorn the Essex county road signs, as well as
the Council letterheads. The word 'Sassenach' too – the derogato-
ry name the Scots use for the English – is from the same root. And
if, as I did, you should ever visit Westphalia in Germany, which was
part of Lower Saxony, you'll find the countryside and the people
not dissimilar in either looks or attitude to those in southern East
Anglia. The Germans liked it here and always have done. Ask the
few local descendants of the German POWs, who never went home
after the war. Earlier too, when an entire regiment of Germans
were stationed in Colchester in 1854, ready for deployment to the
Crimea (in the end, they were never used) many of them married
Colchester girls.

After the Romans pulled out of Britain, the Saxons had it pretty much their own way for a couple of centuries. Many of our country churches are Saxon at core and many of those obscure saints such as Botolph, Runwald and Erconwald bore Saxon names. Then those pesky Norsemen blew in. They raided the east coast every summer. After the first few war parties, whole armies began arriving in longships, laying waste to towns and settlements, taking protection money and often land too. The raids went on for the best part of two centuries, with the English sometimes driving them back to the sea, or at other times, being defeated themselves. Always, though, the Norsemen returned, until finally, we ended up with Canute, a Danish king.

Within a few decades of Canute taking charge, the Normans showed up. Half-Viking and half-Gallic, the acquisitive and efficient Normans made a complete inventory of every pig, duck and two-bit farmhouse they could find. They called their inventory the Domesday Book. It comes in two separate volumes and Essex, along with Suffolk and Norfolk, features in the smaller of the two. It took another couple of hundred years of assimilation, though, before the people of Essex, like much of England, had been smelted into one relatively stable alloy. It had been forged from Teuton, Scandinavian and Frankish – with a good dollop of Romano-Celt at its base.

Much later, between the 16th and 18th centuries, the Flemish weavers and Huguenot refugees arrived at Harwich from Flanders and the Low Countries. These new immigrants were accomplished weavers who manufactured superior cloths called Bays and Says. Colchester's Dutch Quarter is where many of them lived and worked and as a result of these incomers' skills, the town's economy flourished once again through the cloth trade. Surnames such as Boyer, Jordan or LeFevre, still found in the local phonebook are usually of Hueguenot origin. The weavers were also the reason why you'll sometimes see certain town buildings and old farmhouses with Flemish roofs similar to those still seen in the Low Countries today.

The next invasion of north Essex was more stealthy and consisted of lowland Scots farmers who arrived here in the early decades of the 20th century. A surprising number of farmers around the Tendring peninsula bear surnames such as MacDonald, Macaulay, Mitchell, Robertson or Campbell – all of them Scots names. Following two agricultural depressions in the mid and late 19th century, there was a drift of population in north Essex and south Suffolk to the newly industrialised towns. This exodus from the land was partially balanced by a counter-drift southwards of lowland Scots farmers who were prepared to take on cheaper land and, sometimes, derelict farms. With the cruel memories of the Clearances still more or less in living memory at that time, to a rural Scotsman, used to hardship, farming in this region would not have seemed all that hard – as farming goes. The land was good. The climate was even better. Essex today is still generally regarded as the driest and the sunniest of English counties.

The Mitchell Family were probably the earliest Scots settlers in this region. G.K. Mitchell, for instance, came here in 1898 from Linlithgow in the Scottish lowlands. His sons began farming at Great Bentley and Wix. Another branch of the family came to Elmstead in 1912. They're still there today and Ian Mitchell, a descendant, runs a flourishing brick and weatherboard farm shop in Elmstead – a business originally begun from an old horsebox at the side of the road which once sold potatoes and cabbages.

Whether you drive up the A133 to Clacton, or take the train, it's a pretty safe bet that much of the farmland which you'll cross will be owned by someone with a Scots surname, albeit these days, without a Scots accent. The Scots settlers married local girls – and their daughters married local boys. Lowland Scot and North-east Essexman was a formidable farming hybrid. The descendants of that early drift southwards still farm many of the huge swathes of land which you'll see in the north of the county today.

A few years ago I was lucky enough to meet Mrs. MacDonald, a farmer's wife of Great Bentley. By then in her early nineties, she was rather frail, though still as bright as a button, with the most vivid blue eyes. She remembered, as a young girl, attending the now-ruined St. Peter's church at Alresford. Her family once had their own pew there. She also remembered at some point during the Second World War seeing a German plane, a Messerschmitt, come down in flames in the fields on her farm. She described the incident to me. Alone in the house, with her husband elsewhere that day, she grabbed his shotgun and ran out of the building over the fields towards the plane. When she got there, she said, she could see that "the hun" hadn't survived and that people had stopped on the road nearby and were beginning to come over the hedge and run towards the site of the crash. She told me that, feeling rather foolish, she hid the gun in a ditch, to be collected later. She then made her way back to the farmhouse.

She told me this story over the discreet tinkle of teacups, in a rather genteel voice whilst a carer bandaged her foot for her. I suddenly had a very clear, almost psychic picture of a young wartime farmer's wife 'doing her bit' and scarcely even thinking about it. Without being corny, I felt that I was listening to a voice from history – almost a different breed of woman. I sometimes observe the young mums of today wheeling their pushchairs up the road, outside the room where I'm writing this chapter. I try to imagine whether any of them would do such a thing now – just grab the nearest weapon to hand and run towards a crashed burning enemy aircraft in a nearby field, just in case anything needed to be done.

Mrs. Alice Green of Wivenhoe, grand matriarch of the local Green fishing family once told me a similar war story. With her husband away at war, she'd been left on her own with four young sons to bring up: "And venturesome young lads they were too." she told me. There was a dogfight in the sky overhead. A British fighter had engaged a German plane and her boys were keen to see the combat. Alice, realising the danger of the situation, was trying to get them all into the concrete air-raid shelter in the back garden. "As fast as I got two of them down there, another one would pop up and run past me to see what was going on." Again, I had a picture of a doughty wartime wife, struggling to keep her brood from danger, while a dogfight raged overhead and bits of bullet-casing and plane splinters tinkled to earth somewhere nearby.

The last invasion of North Essex, one which has been going on since the 19th century coming of the railways, came from East London. The East Londoners have always held Essex – especially its coast – in some affection. For East London, a tough and once very unhealthy place, Essex has been an escape – almost a wonderland of sorts. In nearly every big city in England, it was usually the east which was the poorer side. There's a reason why this is so. When the industrial revolution arrived, the towns expanded around the filthy factories. The poor were housed cheaply and nearer to their work places. The wealthier people and the factory owners usually built their own dwellings to the west. The prevailing winds in our country are westerly or south-westerly. You don't want the smoke, the smell and the general pollution from the factories blowing over your posh houses, do you? So you build them upwind, to the west, away from the noise and smell. London's West End is one example of this. Nearer to home, in Colchester, the foot of East Hill, the Hythe and even St. Botolphs were where the poor used to live. Leafy Lexden Road to the west, with the posh avenues leading off it, is where you'll find the big houses. I can make this east-west, poor-rich division with a number of other towns and it nearly always fits.

Take a black cab from Liverpool Street to the West End and talk to the driver. Very often, you'll find he knows North Essex. "Wivenhoe? Yeah. I know it. I go fishing in a place not far from there." Or: "We've got a holiday caravan out near St. Osyth." are typical responses. During the summer, for years now, the East End cabbies have run a series of special day trips into Essex for children with special needs. In summer of 1952, Charlie Flemwell, an east London taxi-driver, organised eight black cabs to take a group of such children on an outing to the Essex town of Maldon, on the River Blackwater. The trip was a huge success and over the next few years the scale and fame of the operation grew until it involved up to 160 cabs travelling in convoy with auxiliary buses. The ambulance service would accompany the cabbies for the whole journey and the Metropolitan and Essex police provided a ten-strong motorcycle escort to stop traffic and keep the route clear. The children who came on the outings often had disabilities such as autism, Down's syndrome or severe learning difficulties. Charles Flemwell, who later became Mayor of Newham, died in 1994 but his son Ken carries the tradition on. The East London Cabbies Outing completed its 56th annual Maldon run in 2008 and is still going strong.

"I remember it was always sunny – always really good weather." said Dave Allen, a London cabbie for almost twenty-five years. Dave did the Maldon trip several times. He remembered the balloons festooning each cab and the people who lined Maldon's streets cheering when the convoy arrived. Why Maldon, though? I asked. He didn't really know, he said. But he supposed it was an easier run than say, Clacton or Brighton – although there'd been trips there too. He'd even done a run to Boulogne once. There were also trips for war veterans. The cab drivers, as well as giving their time over to such activities, also paid for their own petrol.

"There'd be three or four kids in each cab, with a carer." Dave recalled. The children were collected from various schools and homes in east London. Dave picked up his young passengers from the Elizabeth Fry School in Canning Town. The convoy left East Ham at 9 a.m., traditionally breaking its journey mid-morning, for an hour-long stop at The George and Dragon pub in Mountnessing. Here the children, many of whom needed special care, were rested and were given any necessary medical treatment before the cabbies pressed on, reaching Maldon by lunchtime. At Maldon's Plume Secondary School, the convoy was met by pupils, staff and the town's mayor, before making its way to the Promenade Park for an afternoon of games and entertainment. There was a prize for the best-dressed cab. "Which I never won," said Dave, " because half of my balloons always seemed to come off before we got there. But it made you feel a bit humble, I suppose. I had little kids myself at the time and you thought: 'There but for the grace of God...'"

Dave Allen, born in Bow sixty years ago and like so many Eastenders who moved to Essex, always had a rather positive view of the county. Like the children who still come to Maldon each year, Essex was his first experience of the countryside. "My dad took me to Romford Cattle Market. I was quite little so it would have been about 1956 or so. It was really open – much different. I hadn't realised it was like that."

The countryside around Romford, though? I considered this. It's a little further out now, yet still very much in evidence. In fact, a casual glance at an ordinary road atlas still reveals substantial stretches of green belt within only about a 20-mile radius of say, Manor Park. And there are probably kids in Bow, Stratford and East Ham now – especially those whose families arrived more recently in the UK – who might never have seen it and may not even be aware of it. And perhaps all the inner-city kids in places like Newham and Canning Town should be bussed out there two or three times a year. Because it's only on their doorstep and heaven knows there's enough room. If I lived in one of those windswept tower-blocks seen from the London train on the way into Liverpool Street and it was all I had to look out at, it would be absolutely great to think that a place like Maldon, wasn't all that far away. Old Charlie Flemwell, the London cabbie, really had something there.

And the Eastenders loved Essex. They didn't think, as certain sniffy urbanites do now, that it was the capital's scruffy backyard – a kind of chavvy scrapheap, full of be-trainered Dazzas racing their Escorts up and down the A12. To Eastenders, past and present, Essex was a holiday land. They could fish, swim, walk, or simply relax in the cheerful caravan resorts, campsites or seaside B&Bs. To a taxi driver or factory hand from Poplar or West Ham, Essex (until the advent of cheap flights and package tours) would have seemed not that far removed from heaven. They too began to settle here. They bought bungalows and ran market stalls in Clacton. They took pubs in some of the villages. They retired to semis in Alresford and Great Bentley, sold cars, applied for allotments or started roadside cafes. When the old East End was knocked down, they moved out to Chadwell Heath, Seven Kings, eventually migrating farther north to estates in Colchester or Braintree. The fusion of cockney and country has given Essex a reputation for no-nonsense toughness – a right-here-right-now attitude found rather less often in the snootier shires and richer southern counties. They moved to sunny Essex because they liked it. They're still coming.

Chapter 5

Train of Thought

I suppose it must have been at sometime in the spring of my twentieth year when I first took that Colchester to Clacton train. It was 1973. I'd just moved from Goldhanger on the River Blackwater to Great Bentley. The trains to Great Bentley ran from St. Botolphs – now re-named Colchester Town – to Clacton, Walton and Frinton. The trip – strange as this may sound to those for whom it's a mundane thing – is one of my favourite rail journeys. For me, it's right up there with the coastal trip round Dawlish in Devon, Weybourne to Holt in Norfolk or the Grosmont to Pickering steam train in North Yorkshire. If I really wanted to give a foreign visitor a good look at the beauty of the north Essex countryside, this might be a good way to start. Each station stop has its own flavour and the intervening countryside, unassuming as it might first seem, is both vast and generous.

Colchester Town, St. Botolophs, or St. Bots if we must, has always been ugly kid brother to the rather statelier Colchester North Station. There used to be an old Polish ticket collector who worked there in the early and mid 1970s. He had a little wartime moustache and an abrupt manner. One day, when a friend of mine – a teenager drummer also of Polish origin – alighted with either the wrong ticket or an extra fare to pay, the ticket collector immediately started giving him a hard time. Hungover after a gig and faced with this bureaucratic onslaught, the drummer said to him blankly: "I'm not scared of *you*. I've had it all my life. My dad's a miserable Polish bastard too."

St. Botolphs has been a place of dispute, discontent and drunken misunderstandings for many, many years now. In the 'seventies as you walked out of the station and turned the corner, The Fountain pub was on your right. A ginger-haired busker called Derek could often be seen sitting in there, playing barrel-house blues on an old piano. He was pretty good at it too, but you didn't generally hang around in there for too long because rather rough men drank in there and fights sometimes broke out.

Just past the pub and around the corner, is a metal sculpture – a machine component of some kind – with a plaque commemorating the Britannia Engineering Works, which once stood where the car park is now. It was destroyed by incendiary bombs in 1944. It had been a busy night for the firemen and the story goes that there wasn't quite enough water in the Jumbo water tower to save it.

The same raid destroyed Bloomfields furniture store too. Three hundred years earlier, St. Botolph's Priory had also taken a severe hammering from Parliamentary cannon, during the Civil War Siege. Earlier still, in mediaeval times, the area was known for its poor people, human dungheaps, bear -baiting and whorehouses.

Even the 12th century St. Botolphs Priory, for the size of it and its premier Augustinian status at the time, was not particularly well heeled as a religious house. Now call me a pessimist if you wish, but I reckon it might be damned ground myself. Strangely, though, I'm sort of fascinated by it and have an abiding affection for the area. St. Botolph's Church, for instance, built in 1835, looms sombrely at passers-by from the bottom of a dark close leading off Queen Street. It was built by the same architect who three years later designed the similarly gothic St. Lawrence's in the village of Rowhedge. Both churches have something of an echo of Nicholas Hawksmoor about them, though the saturnine grandiosity of St. Botolph's seems less incongruously situated than its equally handsome sister church. St. Botolph's Church, though – no matter how foreboding it may appear on the exterior – is renowned for the quality of its music recitals and is actually quite beautiful inside.

In the sunny run-down old mid-1970s, there were strikes galore, the IRA were running a mainland bombing campaign, pop music was at a ghastly standstill and nobody that I knew ever seemed to have any money. The times were as dull as ditchwater. Though, as John Cooper Clarke once said to me: "Ah, but dull is *good*, sometimes, Martin." This being true in many respects, I remember much of the mid-seventies as a rather relaxed, carefree sort of time. The scruffy old local trains pulled out of St. Botolphs in summer and rattled between weed-choked embankments, where the bindweed twined prettily over broken fences. Then they crossed the river over the East Bay allotments until they came to the twenty acres of urban wilderness known as the Moors. In late summer, the Moors were and still are particularly attractive. The reeds grow high by the muddy Colne and the ranks of rosebay willowherb stand up like gangs of Red Indian braves among the deep green foliage and long summer grasses.

A cycle path runs through the Moors now and yet, whenever you go along it, you'll hardly ever see anyone else there. During my own childhood, such a place might have been teeming with kids making dens or fishing for tiddlers. I sometimes get the impression, however, that its very wildness is what makes people wary of it. Maybe, in our jittery and safety-conscious times, the parents don't want their kids playing there. The people's loss, however, is the wildlife's gain. The Moors area is alive with lizards and newts, the bee-wolf wasp, grass-snakes, birds, toads and all manner of other species. It's recognised as a wildlife haven now but apart from the odd dog-walker and cyclist, for an area surrounded on all sides by human activity, most of the time it's still relatively deserted.

The trains then creaked and groaned their way into Hythe station, for many years a run down place of coal-heaps, rusty girders, old rails and ragwort. For here had been the old industrial heartland of Colchester. Here also were the factory yards, including Colchester Lathes – once famous throughout the world – piles of oil drums, scrapyards, old vehicles and all the detritus and death rattles of the dying industrial age. It wasn't pretty but it was tremendously interesting. I've sort of haunted the Hythe over the years, even when it's been rough and run down. When I first knew the place in early 1971, aged 17, it was still very much a working dock. The ships sailed in, the trucks rolled out and the pubs were full of tough and tired looking men. At lunchtimes in summer, you might see men sitting outside on the wall, eating their rolls or smoking and reading tabloids. From the dirty moaning old trains, you'd catch other views too: the river at high or low tide in the dog days of August, when the air was thick with thistledown 'fairies' drifting around on still, endless afternoons.

The Hythe is a confluence of road, rail and river. This, remember, is one of Colchester's oldest areas. It has an extraordinary psycho-geography as well as a history. It's always been a place of work and vigorous human activity. The Hythe itself was once full of coal boats, water taxis, lighters and grain ships. All around the area is industry overlaid upon industry. Over the same marshland that the Saxons and Normans might have known, came the wrought iron railway girders of Victorian enterprise and, by the station itself, were the piles of coal that fuelled most of its activity. Of all the areas in Colchester earmarked for regeneration, though, the Hythe is probably the one with the pedigree and location to make a successful transition, because there's always been something going on there.

Back on the old trains, meanwhile, there was a quick chug across the Hythe level crossing and the last bits of the eastern outskirts rattled by until the terrain changed once again. Now, you found yourself looking out at the river on the right and some marshy fields to the left, with the University towers standing guard over it all, up on the gentle slopes. Here, the river began to widen and with the beginning of Wivenhoe Woods to the right, you might be lucky, at high tide to glimpse a large German or Danish ship on its way down to the Hythe Docks. Nowadays, since the docks at Rowhedge, Wivenhoe and Hythe have stopped working, you don't see the big boats any more, though you do occasionally catch sight of a Thames barge in full sail. Don't get me wrong: a Thames barge is a lovely thing but it's become for the heritage industry, a waterborne equivalent of a thatched beamed cottage. A Thames barge is majestic and pretty and some people just love going on them on Sundays and standing in their Croc shoes, eating ciabattas and waving at the shore. Me? I'd rather see a dirty old trawler guffing its way upriver again, with a hold full of fish and an unshaven, poker-faced old skipper at the wheel.

Before the new waterfront housing estate was built, it was possible sometimes, to stand on Wivenhoe Station, gazing across the marshes opposite and see only the top half of a massive ship moving slowly past nearby. As you couldn't see the river itself from this point, it was a surrealistic sight. In fact it was redolent of an early scene in Hitchock's film, *Marnie*, where a large ship looms at the bottom of a suburban street, whilst girls play a skipping game in the immediate foreground.

After a slam of doors, a whistle and a shout, the train pulled out of Wivenhoe, picking up speed under the Anglesea Road bridge where the countryside opens up, revealing John Bowes' fields and copses. Beyond them is a view of the ever-widening Colne Estuary. Soon you'd reach Alresford and the back gardens of the dullish suburban houses built in the Sixties and Seventies. The stations all the way up to Clacton are still fairly sleepy places and the line is punctuated by several newly automated level crossings. The station buildings themselves are pleasing, if run-down Victorian creations which once accommodated station masters and their families. It was a perfectly good notion having stationmasters living in such places. It housed the staff, made sure that the stations were always manned and probably gave the passengers a sense that someone was looking after them.

Was it cost-effective? It must have been at one time, since the system seems to have worked for years. Until somebody somewhere decided that perhaps it didn't. The result, tortuous decades later, is that some of the stations now have only a part-time ticket office or worse, machine-only ticketing. The live-in stationmasters are long-gone and the level crossing keepers have recently been dispensed with too. An electronic voice tells passengers which, if any trains are due in. Security cameras now scan the platforms and if there are persistent problems during the evening with 'Da Yoof', the police will perform an occasional purge. These changes are known as 'efficiencies' or 'improvements.' Sometimes, the entire local rail network may be closed for up to three days at a time, in order to carry out such improvements. I get the impression that it all works extremely well – as long as no actual passengers are involved in the procedure.

It's on the approach to Alresford, past Thorrington, where the fields begin to slope and roll a bit more and you'll notice horse paddocks, woods and the wider farmlands. And then you come to Great Bentley. Great Bentley has a vast village green that is sometimes credited as being the biggest in England. There's speculation that a bigger one exists somewhere in Nottinghamshire. though, because I have a life, I've never bothered trying to confirm the fact.

Bentley Green itself is surrounded by large and elegant houses, some of them built in the classic Georgian provincial style found so often in this part of Essex. And no, you don't want to go and live in one. What would be the point, now? You'd have twenty years struggling with the garden, before you'd have to scrape up the money for a Stannah stair-lift and then a final decline into living in two rooms downstairs. The only thing you'd end up looking forward to by then would probably be a morning chat with the home help in a big echoey kitchen that smelled of last night's microwave meal and an un-riddled Aga. Sure the houses look great from the outside. But forget them. What you really need is a nice bungalow up the road in Aingers Green. That's where my mum lives.

One of the hidden charms of Great Bentley Green, tucked away in one corner, is a beautiful little village pond, complete with pretty white railings. It's the kind of thing that you might find, on the June page of a Village England calendar that your auntie sent you at Christmas. If I'm over there on the bike, it's where I'll generally stop to eat my lunch. It occurred to me, however, that it would probably also make a thoroughly good place to stand and stare at wistfully, on a partially cloudy day in September, following the unexpected break-up of a marriage.

Great Bentley, when I first knew it, had several shops and three pubs: The Plough, The Red Lion and The Victory. Of the pubs, The Victory and The Red Lion are long gone. Most of the little shops are gone too, replaced by a Tesco Express, now standing where Symonds – a really wonderful hardware store – used to be. The Great Bentley cricket ground, which is part of the green, also has an unusual feature. The players have to walk out of the pavilion and cross a road in order to be able go out to bat.

Great Bentley station used to be one of the prettiest in the county and for years after the war nearly always won the Best-Kept Station awards. The place was manned by a cheerful Scots railman called Jock who sold tickets, opened and closed the gates and swept the platforms. I also seem to remember flower beds on the Colchester side and even, a small goldfish pond. People these days sometimes think you're a bit peculiar if you start waxing nostalgic about old country stations, but some of them, a few decades ago, were uniquely pleasant places, with coal fires in waiting rooms, as well as serviceable and *unlocked* loos. A goldfish pond on a station platform? It seems almost unimaginable now. Though, I believe that it's the gradual removal of exactly such eccentrically civilising touches which has helped to coarsen the English as a people. This is well illustrated, when something vaguely re-humanising occurs, however momentarily, in a modern situation.

At Wivenhoe Station last winter, for instance, a cat took to coming into the ticket hall and sleeping on one of the seats. Soon enough, a cushion found its way onto the seat and the cat could be seen sleeping upon it, or, on waking, being made a fuss of by various passengers. It transformed the feel of the room. People mired in the tedium and insecurity of rail travel love such things. Goldfish ponds, flower beds, a station house with a family living in it and a cat on a seat somewhere. They were all great ideas. All manner of inefficiencies and delays might be softened by such things if they were to be reinstated today. You could get rid of all of those security cameras, flashing electronic bulletin boards, those silly automated announcements and no one would really mind. People just want to feel *looked after* when they're travelling. This, unfortunately, is rarely the case nowadays. Ask a government expert and he or she will tell you that the old railways used to lose money. Though, they did used to *work* – sort of. And you didn't generally embark on a train journey with a vague sense of trepidation or even dread, wondering: "*Now* what?" Nor did you accept that for large chunks of the year, at weekends especially, the train that you'd paid for would actually be a bus. Our current rail travel system is actually a type of madness – an infuriating and inglorious madness in which we have become complicit, by allowing it to impede our lives and livelihoods.

Chapter 6

Panto Isolating Cock

On the old Eastern Region trains, if I put my bicycle in the guard's van, I'd sometimes see an arrow somewhere up on the wall at the end of the carriage. Above it, usually hand-written, was the phrase: *Panto Isolating Cock*. I have had endless fun over the years, wondering what it meant and concocting jokes to do with what it might have been. I'm not going to rake back over them now, but readers are free to tinker with the phrase themselves. An old train driver did once tell me what a panto isolating cock actually did but I've forgotten again now. I think, however, it was something to do with the braking system on older locomotives.* Sadly I have never seen the words "panto isolating cock" on any of the new trains.

The next station after Great Bentley is Weeley, for me, still indelibly stained into my memory as the site of the famous 1971 pop festival. Practically everybody I knew at the time went to Weeley. For various reasons, I actually didn't. Weeley, in some ways, became a sort of milder British equivalent of the Altamont festival in America. Altamont, of course, was the fin-de-siècle American rock event where the American Hells Angels beat and knifed a man to death – and where the Rolling Stones were lucky to get out more or less unscathed.

At the Weeley Festival, however, depending upon whom you listen to, our own Hells Angels came off rather badly. For some time the Angels had been employed as a sort of unofficial security firm for our then largely unregulated and un-policed pop festivals. The strange hippy-biker alliance had come about after punters attending certain pop concerts in London had found themselves being menaced by first generation 1969 era skinheads. In a grudge match that

---

* The 'Panto Isolating Cock' is a control to enable the train's guard to disconnect the power-collecting pantograph from the overhead power lines in the event of an emergency. The pantograph (the coat hanger thingy on top of the train carriage) is held against the power lines by air pressure. In the event of an emergency, the air supply would be cut off and the pantograch would descend, disabling the train. In the event of this not happening, the train's guard can cut off the air supply by shutting the 'Panto Isolating Cock' in his van, thus causing the pantograph to descend and removing (or at least reducing) the danger of electrocution.

had carried over from the mods and rockers' battles, the Hells
Angels and bikers became natural enemies of the reggae-loving
skinheads. Predominantly working-class themselves they were
unlike the hippies, though they possessed long-haired outlaw status
and enjoyed similar forms of music. Placing the peace-loving mid-
dle-class hippies, however, in the same recreational space as the
party-loving roughneck bikers wasn't a comfortable arrangement.
In fact it was akin to parking a large alsation dog next to a nervous
Persian cat with only the instruction " Good boy. Now guard!" This
uneasy relationship between silk and leather, however, had more or
less worked – up until the time of the Weeley Pop Festival. For it was
at Weeley where the wheels finally came off.

It had all started with a bit of silliness, as is so often the case, but
this time it ended in tears. The Angels, it was said at the time, had
'borrowed' a security jeep and were riding around the festival
ground in it, generally larking around. The tough London hot-dog
stallholders, along with some real security people – many of them
reportedly ex-commandos – decided that it was time to teach the
feisty Angels a lesson. They marched en masse to where the bikers
were grouped and began to smash their bikes up. When the Hells
Angels reacted, they were beaten savagely with pick-axe handles,
boots and fists, in what may well have been a pre-planned attack.

Some of the bikers, who might have seemed terrifying if you
were only a skinny sixteen year-old hippie at the time, were actually not much more than teenage boys themselves. They were certainly no match for an organised, tooled-up force of London thugs and
former soldiers. The under-manned Essex police, with their hands
now full, allegedly allowed the ad-hoc security force a certain
amount of leeway for their vigilantism before scooping the remaining Angels up and carting them off either to hospital, or to the nick.
A friend of mine who was a band-roadie at the time, with not much
love himself for the biker gangs, told me that what had happened to
the Angels was disgraceful. Many had skull fractures and other serious injuries. One of the bikers allegedly died later, although this was
never confirmed. Many prized customised bikes were destroyed or
damaged and along with them, to an extent, the fearsome pride of
the Hells Angels. The local media reports weren't exactly sympathetic either and showed bikers lying unconscious and bloodied next
to their ruined machines. You could almost say that this was the

point at which red-neck entrepreneurialism first bared its ugly teeth at what had essentially become a free counter-culture event.

The crushed-velvet era was now threadbare and even if I wasn't at that particular event, I do remember the gone stale atmosphere of the time all too well. It was possibly after the 1971 Weeley Festival that the so-called English hippie underground began to get over itself and finally let go of the 1960s. A year or so after the Weeley Festival, my parents moved out to nearby Aingers Green and I visited the old site. It was my own Pilgrimage of Regret I suppose. I stood there wistfully in the wind blowing over the autumn fields, like it was the week after Custer's Last Stand. I don't know what I'd expected to find. The fluting of distant pan-pipes and a broken guitar neck sticking out of the stubble, perhaps? A rusting old Watney's Party Four tin and a fragment of paisley shirt? There was nothing. It was just a bit of farmland up the road. It was also a chunk of my lost youth. And Jimi Hendrix was dead. August? Yep. It would have been about that time of year.

Now the train jerked and, with a crick of its axles, left Weeley, accelerating towards Thorpe-le-Soken. Thorpe-le-Soken station used to be one of my favourite places. It's here where you change for Walton on the Naze, Kirby Cross and Frinton – or Clacton, if you happen to be on a Walton train.

Numberless Eastenders in the long decades before cheap foreign travel would have briefly disembarked here on the way to the seaside. Here they stood, liberated from the cramped dirty city at last, chattering and smoking, or sitting on battered leather cases like refugees, gazing all around at the country station. Below the platform on the station's far side, was an old house with a long garden. The bottom of the garden was overgrown in summer and in a small clearing, wild rabbits could sometimes be seen hopping around and feeding.

On the ticket-office side, just beyond the fence, were Thorpe Maltings, which made the malt for *Double Diamond* beer. On certain days, the smell of malt pervaded the whole station area and it seemed to cling to your nostrils long after the train had departed. Just by the station yard was the King Edward pub, The Ted, as locals called it. The Ted was a magnificent old Edwardian boozer, situated on a bit of greensward where a large horse chestnut tree grew. Adorning its first floor were a couple of flouncy white metal balconies, whose curlicues had the effect of making the building look like it was wearing a big white lacy brassiere. The builders had cut no corners and the gents' toilets, too, were in extravagant period tradition, with large vitreous china urinals, surrounded by good tiling. It's probably a strange thing to say, but you just don't see that kind of quality in pub toilets anymore. The Ted, if you see it now, is very run down and abandoned looking.

At some point during the Nineties, after the pub had closed its doors for the last time, it became a nightclub with the charming name, "Bonkers". It reportedly hosted all manner of the fun and shenanigans, which you might imagine a venture of such a description would afford. It didn't last very long. At time of writing, scrap dealers now occupy the old Ted and there are piles of wrecked cars sitting next to it. At least someone's using the place, which is better than it being totally abandoned. The lacy white bra metalwork on the balconies is tarnished and brown and the building looks generally unloved. The horse chestnut tree is still there though, but looks rather forlorn in its new setting among the uncut grasses of late summer.

The King Edward, you see, was all part of the charm of Thorpe's Monday Market, which I first began going to in the mid-1970s. The market hosted fruit and flower auctions in one rusting old iron shed and a second-hand household goods auction in an adjacent one. The auctioneer often presiding there was himself a sort of throwback to another time. He wore a smart country jacket, spoke in a clipped "Heppy dahling?" accent and peered imperiously over half-moon specs at the crowd, whilst he flogged them boxes of marigolds, turnips and tomato plants. He had something of Kenneth More about him and gave the impression that he'd have probably been happier thirty years earlier, dufflecoated on the bridge of a naval patrol boat with a pair of binoculars and a mug of cocoa. I loved to watch and listen to him work. Even as a relatively shallow young whip in my early twenties I knew, somehow, that when that particular generation of Englishmen died out, they'd probably never be replaced.

If you were a bit hard up, which I constantly was as a young man, Thorpe Market was where you went to acquire all the practical stuff that you needed, cheaply. You could pick up a working vacuum cleaner there, or various gadgets and widgets for your house or garden. The bric-a-brac of the entire 20th century, it seemed, had ended up at Thorpe Market. Here you could buy re-conditioned tools, gaffer-tape, mixed nails in a bag, old car spares and much else. The stallholders were equal parts Cockney and Essex countryfolk and they all seemed to rub along together just fine. The only thing was, that if you wanted the real bargains you'd have to get there at sometime around 7 a.m. – a bit of a tall order in those days for rock-'n'roll kiddies who were fond of staying up late. Having got there early, though, you wouldn't starve or anything. There was a coffee and bacon sandwich stall too. Best of all was the King Edward, which opened its doors early so that you could sit there and have a pint of beer, while listening to the market-traders talking about their gains and losses. On a gusty and bright October morning, with a damp westerly blowing through the rusty trees, when the station-yard was crowded with punters and stalls, there was nothing finer than observing it all from the bustling old King Edward. Then, all the while, the trains rolled in and out between Clacton and Colchester adding to the feeling of constant bustle.

With the advent of car-boot sales, which in effect, much of Thorpe Market – once actually a livestock market – had become, the event became less popular and gradually ceased to be. The maltings, once mooted as ripe for conversion to yuppie apartments, are now in a state of serious disrepair and are surrounded by make-safe scaffolding. Thorpe le Soken itself is still well worth a visit though. It has a flavour and a feel all its own, with some fabulous old houses and many more large old trees along its main drag than you would generally see in other villages around this area. Buried somewhere in Thorpe's churchyard is Sir William Gull, Queen Victoria's surgeon, who at various times has been suspected of being the real Jack the Ripper. Goths, Johnny Depp fans and the sillier types of amateur detectives – 'Ripperologists' as they sometimes call themselves– will sometimes be seen combing the gravestones for anything that a century of expert forensic science might so far have missed.

Up the road from the station, hidden down a long drive, stood, until a few years ago, the 18th century-built Thorpe Hall, stately residence of four generations of the Leake family. Between the wars, it became the home of Viscount Byng of Vimy – 'Bungo' to his friends. It was purchased towards the end of the Great War, in his absence, by the distinguished warrior's wife. Lady Byng was a woman of formidable energies, who immediately set to work restoring the rambling gardens, clearing the lakes and planting trees. Lady Byng also had one hell of an address book. Frequent visitors to Thorpe Hall during the inter-war years included Winston Churchill, Queen Mary, Princess Alice of Athlone, J.M.Barrie, Rudyard Kipling and many other luminaries. Barrie, Kipling and Churchill all had their own favourite corners of the grounds where, in the comparative lull between the two storms of world war, they'd sit and relax. A statue of Peter Pan stood on a plinth overlooking the lawns at one time, but was stolen some years ago. After a post-war period as a private rest home, Thorpe Hall eventually fell into disrepair for many years, neglected, overgrown and vandalised. With its roof and structure permanently damaged by the elements, the building itself was demolished a few years ago, although some of the older outbuildings remain. Under its new owner, Martin Wooton – an inspired gardener and successful businessman – these buildings now function as a health spa while an ambitious new building is completed. The gardens, fourteen acres of which have been replanted and reclaimed over past years, are an epic adventure in restoration, a project similar in ambition to the much-larger Lost Gardens of Heligan in Cornwall.

For about half a century, just down the road from Thorpe, at Landemere Quay, lived Eduardo Paolozzi, who is often credited as England's first Pop Artist. If you think you don't know his work, you probably do, because if you've ever been to Tottenham Court Road tube station, all the mosaic work on the platforms and in the transit halls is Paolozzi's. Sir Eduardo, as he later became, had three daughters. The eldest was called Louise and she once used to prep the vegetables in the same restaurant on Colchester's North Hill where I was the porter. Just like me, she sometimes took the train. In fact, in the mid-1970s the Colchester-Clacton train was full of famous connections. I'd meet the singer Sade's brother Banji, travelling in to college from Clacton. Davey Payne, Ian Dury's sax player, who lived in Clacton, also took the train down to London sometimes. On rare occasions, you might even see Nicky Hopkins, the skinny session pianist for The Who and The Rolling Stones. When he wasn't on tour he sometimes travelled out to Frinton to see his parents. You'd meet Louise's sisters Emma and Anna. And back then you'd also meet me, a long-haired young nonentity from Aingers Green, on his way to either a day's washing-up or a night's singing in some dodgy club. It was *that* kind of a train. Though I must repeat, just one last time: Panto isolating cock.

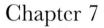

Chapter 7

Colchester – *Rockin' and Ruckin'*

Colchester is a town of many layers. In its way, the place is almost as complex and mysterious as London. And yet, no one, so far as I know, has ever bothered to write a psycho-geography of the place and no chansonnier or rocker has ever bothered to eulogise it in song. But the town has a few things wrong with it too. So long as I've known it, there's been a grass-roots negativity to be found in certain quarters – a feeling common to many English provincial towns that nothing good has come out of it and nothing ever will. Young guys in rock bands who read too many music newspapers mumble sullenly that there's no chance of getting anywhere in this town. And yet, when someone does manage to break out, make a record, pick up a bit of acclaim, the general levels of rancour in the town's music venues rise palpably. Damon Albarn, reportedly, stopped coming back here after Blur became famous, because every time he went into a pub to have a drink with his old mates, someone would have a go at him. Very Colchester, that is.

But Colchester has always produced more than its fair share of good rock bands and in the 1960s and 1970s, major acts used to play here too. The Stones, Pink Floyd, The Who and Free all came; and later, during the punk period, many major bands played at Essex University. John Martyn played concerts here almost every year. Woods Social Club put on gigs by Mud, Suzie Quatro and many others. Colchester Institute booked consistently good up-and-coming acts during this time, once securing the Electric Light Orchestra. I have lost count of the number of brilliant bands whom I was lucky enough to be able to see locally when I was young – and when it desperately mattered to me. So far as rock culture was concerned back then, Colchester was most definitely on the tour map.

Of those local musicians who didn't make it, many carried on playing. It's still possible today to go into pubs and clubs all around the area and see middle-aged duos, four-pieces and other acts of exceptionally high quality who really deserve to have done better. But that's the fickle music biz for you. There are lots of people who'd like the job. There's a lot of talent. Everyone wants to be the singer of the song. Perhaps this is because, as Walter Pater once said, "All art aspires to the condition of music." The music business, though, it is well attested, is a chamber of broken dreams and Colchester, no less than anywhere else, has its fair share of former contenders who never felt the wind change and just got stuck that way.

Colchester, unlike Norwich or Ipswich, possibly feels itself not far enough away from the Metropolis to be secure in its own identity and yet not close enough to it to bask in London's self-generated glow of importance. The capital greedily sucks talent from the provinces, gradually drip-feeding it back in one watered-down form or another. It is, after all, what capitals do.

This process is well illustrated by one recent feature of Colchester's music culture. It comes in the form of the municipal music event. For almost two decades, various would-be organisers fought for the opportunity to hold open-air rock events in Castle Park. Such events rarely happened. Councillors shook their heads and vetoed the suggestion. When the authorities, realising that they might make money, finally did light upon the idea of open-air events, it was modelled on the type of thing once organised for corporate entertainments.

Typically, such a concert will consist of an ABBA tribute band, a Queen tribute band and a feel-good 1960s or 1970s package act, with salient local acts occasionally being allowed a low-paid support slot. Tributes are big business. The municipal event is rooted in *giving-the-people-only-what-they-already-know*. And yes, they *do* work, to an extent. Put on such an event in the town park, throw in a few food stalls, a bit of face painting and a few bouncy castles for the kids and then finish the night with some fireworks.

Now get your local papers to promote it all under banner headlines with the words 'Fun' and 'Success' in them. What have you got then: a 'successful' 'fun' event? bigger bouncy castles? Yes. You get Bouncy Castle Park, in fact. At the risk of being called an elitist bore though, what you *haven't* got is culture. The promoters, the council and the people themselves are mired in a kind of cultural karaoke. There's a feeling that if you stick with Freddie, Bjorn, Agnetha, the Sixties and the Seventies that you'll somehow be all right. The menu runs: *Prawn cocktails to start, karaoke and chips for main course and*

fireworks to finish. Never gonna change. It's the people's choice.
Meanwhile, the ghetto-ised fans of indie rock, country, folk, soul
and jazz will always muddle through on their own, increasingly
holding the 'minority' events that the many people really *do* want.
This is why the independent festivals which have sprung up in
Brightlingsea, Mersea, Kelvedon, Wivenhoe and elsewhere have
become so popular during the past few years. The Colchester area
is rich in music and pop-culture of all genres. You just have to find
it and then organise the events for yourselves.

Colchester, though, can get rough sometimes. On weekend
nights, many of the town centre pubs become youth drinking venues – complete with doormen on their entrances sporting radio-mic
earpieces. There are fast food venues, whose wrappings and
remains end up littering the streets in the small hours. On the busier
nights, the police find that they have their hands full keeping order
among the fighting, squawking, vomiting revellers. When the local
papers are published, they are rich with accounts of broken windows, kicked vehicles, youths who've been attacked and men who've
resisted arrest. Reports of court cases following such misde-
meanours nearly always quote the defence that the accused's behaviour was out of character, that an amount of alcohol had been con-
sumed prior to the offence, or that he had been trying to come to
terms with his alcohol or drug misuse – which of course, he had
now put behind him. It is classic hometown 'good night out' stuff.
As the subsequent handwringing ensues in the council chambers
and on the letters pages of the local papers, the conclusion is nearly always that things are getting worse.

Since Boudicca torched Colchester in AD 61 – probably even
before that – Colchester, or a certain aspect of it has always been
Punch-up Central. It's what happens with all English market towns
when young fellows and, increasingly, young women frantically
chug back loads of cut-price alcohol at weekends. They fight,
dance, scream, swear, litter the streets and screw like alley cats. They
will especially do this if there are lots of bars – set up by business-
men and licensed by the local council – which will assist and even
encourage them to get drunk enough to do such things in the first
place. It doesn't help that mainstream TV channels, from mid-
evening onwards, are full of programmes showing our beleaguered
national police forces dealing with exactly such excesses. It has

become the norm. Colchester, however, is no worse than any other town of a similar type. Drunken disorder is a national malaise.

It's been observed, however, that such disorder *does* dissuade other sections of society from entering the town centre on certain nights of the week. This can have a deleterious effect on other aspects of the local economy and culture. One hot summer night, for instance, I was in a taxi coming home from a gig at Colchester Arts Centre. There were people staggering all over the street, following an international football match, which had been televised in the pubs. England had scored. Our taxi became stuck, briefly, among the ecstatic crowds of revellers in the High Street. A drunk boy wrapped in a St. George's flag, lurched over to us, stuck his head through the cab driver's window and bawled "Hoot your horn for England, Mate!" The driver, hands clenched to the driving wheel, eyes straight ahead, repeated tersely. "Get your hands *off* my car." The boy eventually withdrew and staggered back towards a bar. Out in the streets, girls were screaming, falling over and swigging from bottles. The scene was Hogarthian. I would not have wished to be an elderly theatregoer making my way down the High Street at that point in the proceedings. I was glad I was in a taxi and on my way home.

Colchester, of course, has been a garrison town for about two thousand years and became England's biggest garrison town during the Napoleonic era. One of the most common things that Colchester's Wild West reputation is errantly blamed upon is the soldiery: "It's because of the squaddies," they'll tell you. I've lost count of the amount of times I've heard it. Even my mum, a former army wife, says it. But although it's commonly repeated, I just don't believe that the matter is that simple. When you have a market town that is surrounded by rural villages – as Colchester is – the young gladiators will always come in to drink and fight. Add to this, the fact that during the post-war era, large ill-catered for housing estates sprang up on Colchester's flanks to cope with an exodus from London. There has been a huge growth in the town's population during the past few decades. You must also take into account a desperate drinks industry, a disproportionate number of premises geared to binge drinking and a recent change in national licensing laws. Now all you have to do is stir in some nasty drugs, marinade it all in a vat of youthful energy and it's not difficult to see what will happen. Though to be fair, as I've already mentioned, it's not just Colchester where it occurs. It's happening all over the UK. To blame the soldiers though? It's not them. They're easily dealt with. If they cause too much mayhem, these days, they can be confined to barracks. Try doing that with every inebriated 19 year-old civilian arrested this weekend and there'll be a civil rights issue.

Though, it actually *was* quieter in Colchester a few decades ago. I can remember for instance, getting the last London train to Colchester North one Friday night during the autumn of 1976. Round about midnight, I walked home to East Hill from the station and the town was nearly dead. Apart from the odd taxi and a few cars, the only other person I saw on the High Street was a solitary middle-aged drunk staggering home by himself. There were no late-night drinking places back then. I'd been told several times that the reason for this was the fault of the Black Watch. They'd been stationed here a few years earlier and their legendary fighting and drinking had, allegedly, managed to get every club in the town closed down. I've remained unconvinced. I think it was merely a case of old-fashioned councillors in an old-fashioned town keeping a steadier hand on the tiller, as councillors all over the country had been used to doing during that period.

Sure, the town boys took on the young soldiers from time to time and probably always had done. There'd been periodic punch-ups, for instance, in the late 1960s, between the Headgate 'hippies' and the soldiers who drank in The Bull over the road. The hippies – actually not just hippies but a fearsome mixture of bikers, former soldiers, dockers and sundry other bohemian roughnecks – took on some young soldiers who'd been foolish enough to invade the place. It was often the soldiers who came off worst. My own experience of soldiers fighting in pubs, is that it often turns out to be inter-regimental rivalry, or simply, bad blood between soldiers in the same units. In 1973 I saw fights between rival biker groups too. And as if that wasn't enough, years ago you might have been unlucky enough to be in a place where some fishermen from one town met some fishermen from another town. This type of antipathy often went back not years, but generations. And so it went on and on and on. And probably always has done and always will. If you want it, you'll find it, as they say. But it wasn't – and still *isn't* going on all the time everywhere. So why *do* people fight? Drink, we must suppose. Oh, that and the fact that some of them just seem to like it, that's all.

Colchester, however, is worth far more than its reputation for hard drinking and rucking. To me it's become a rather mystical place, full of hidden historical secrets It's also become rather like a parent whom I might have been at odds with during my youth, but whom I've gradually learned to understand and respect. I now think of Colchester as a place that has helped shape me – given me a reslience and cut-to-the-bone way of looking at things which I might, whether I knew it or not, once have needed. It doesn't belong to me, exactly, though as I get older and peel back the layers, I begin to think that I might belong to *it*.

Chapter 8

Da Yoof

In an old Wivenhoe Society newsletter, a few years ago, one of the matters arising was entitled something along the lines of: "What shall we do about our wayward youth?" Youngsters had been congregating outside the Co-op, making a noise on the King George V playing fields, drinking, smoking dope and generally doing all the things that youngsters nowadays seem to do. The question arising in the newsletter had a hand-wringing, tremulous, we'll-all-be-murdered-in-our- beds tone to it. Today, there's a widely held perception that our young have never been so out of control or ill-mannered and that we are witnessing the collapse of civilisation. So what *shall* we do about our wayward youth? For those of you who haven't had yours delivered yet, there's a council telephone number you can ring. The rest of you, come this way.

Whenever I begin to despair of a situation, firstly, I look at the past, to see if there's any precedent for our current woes. There always is, it's nearly always worse and usually, it's not even *that* far back in the past. A hundred years ago for instance, two Colchester boys were up before the beak for throwing stones at people's windows. The magistrate weighed up the case, before having them birched. This happened right in the middle of the long Edwardian afternoon – a *Railway Children*-era that many of us like to fuzzily think of as being somehow more genteel and well-ordered than the present one.

At the time of writing this chapter, Wivenhoe, like many other communities, perceives itself as suffering a certain amount of delinquent behaviour at the hands of the young. The area just outside the Co-op seems to have been the focal point for this. At the peak of it, about 120 to 150 youths arrived one Friday night in various states of inebriation and began taunting and skirmishing with each other. The girls among them egged them on, occasionally joining in. They ranged in age from about 13 years of age, to their early 20s. The lower part of the town seemed briefly to be full of young people shouting, staggering, running and generally being a nuisance. As

I stepped out of my house, later that evening, for a quiet pint round the corner, I was aware of a charged atmosphere in the High Street. Small groups of boys were hanging around. One boy was sitting drunkenly on a windowsill by Rollo's, the estate agents. Another was calling to him and urging him to hurry up, because *something* or other had to be done about *something* soon. Three drunk girls – rather the other side of fashionably slim – had got into a pickle of some sort further down the street: one had broken her shoe, another was falling over and a third had dropped her pint glass in somebody's "effin' garden." In the pub, I was told there'd been a 'bit of trouble' in the Indian restaurant – this turned out to be one or two scared youths taking panicky refuge there, during a pursuit by a larger group of boys.

As I left the pub, one rapidly gargled pint later, the earlier charged atmosphere had dissipated somewhat. Six policemen were now standing at the park gates opposite. A police helicopter was puttering anxiously around overhead. The evening began to settle down. At closing time though, there were still four policemen, stretched in a small cordon across the town car park exit. During the time I'd been in the pub, there had been what the police chiefs, whom we see on TV nowadays, refer to as 'a robust response.'

The summer of 2007 had seen a series of incidents involving truculent youths congregating at the railway station on otherwise pleasant evenings. Complaints by locals had eventually led to a similarly robust police response, with constables using an 'appropriate' amount of force, reportedly, on one young blade, who was pinioned face-down, handcuffed and lifted horizontally into a police van still screaming threats and abuse at his captors. The regulars in the nearby Station Hotel, one or two of whom had themselves been threatened during previous incidents that summer, came out and watched the robust response with delight, barely suppressing a standing ovation as the youths were forcibly removed from the scene.

A few months later, one quiet midweek afternoon, I was in the Post Office doing some photocopying. A boy, who'd been staggering around in the street with two of his mates, lurched roughly in, peered into the cold drinks refrigerator and slurred loudly: "Naaa...fugghin'..they 'int got none." He asked Alan, the postmaster, something or other and Alan, disapprovingly, shook his head. I looked at the boy. He was about sixteen years old, ginger haired, with a Russian drunk-tank haircut and red-rimmed, angry, out-of-it eyes. He was shirtless. He looked hot, bewildered, stoned and drunk. It was about three o'clock in the afternoon. As they slouched off up the street in an untidy straggle I muttered brightly to myself: "Lovely!"

Go into certain pubs where young people congregate on Friday nights, and they can get very noisy indeed. As they bellow into their mobile phones, the conversations are rich with expletives and belches. They also chug back strong lagers and strange cerise-coloured vodka-based drinks, as if to indicate that their lives depended upon it. Many of the lads are hulking and, sometimes, rather flabby. The girls, with their straightened peroxide hair, blank eyes and WAG clothing styles, will usually match the boys, drink for drink, expletive for expletive. So where *did* all these huge, coarse and drunken young strangers suddenly spring from?

Unsurprisingly, most of them are actually Wivenhoe's children. They went to Broomgrove and Millfields Primary schools and thereafter to the Colne School, or to other schools in Colchester. Only a few years ago, many of them were those elfin little creatures taking part in crabbing competitions on the town Quay, or keenly pedalling BMX bicycles around the streets. What are they really *like* though? If you should ever get into conversation with them during an earlier, quieter part of the evening, you might discover that one lad runs a removal business, another is training to be a brickie and a third wants to join the RAF. A few of them have musical ambitions, do a bit of deejaying or play guitar – usually in Indie bands. Ask their female counterparts and similarly, you may find that the girl wearing the unduly heavy foundation make-up is a trainee nursery nurse, that a second, with her watery gun-grey eyes is at college, studying architecture and that a third one, currently drunk and lost in (texting) space, helps to run an office for her dad. They mostly go to work and are doing scarily normal stuff for a living. That is, they are when they're not out on the lash, being professionally rowdy and putting furry old baby-boomers off their Pinots.

Now *you* may have formed your own preconceptions about them but they, too, have formed theirs about you. To them, you might be a boring old lecturer, a useless deadbeat artist, or just some old no-mark, too steeped in your own dull world to interface, in any way, with their own fast-paced youthful delirium. If, however, you bother to talk to them and they suddenly discover that you know their dad and think well of him, or that their mum used to hang out with your crowd, decades ago, the inter-generational ice may begin to thaw slightly. It won't make all of you bosom buddies or anything, but it may stop *them* from arming themselves with surface belligerence every time you pass each other in the corridor. And it may stop *you* looking like a fusty disapproving old git every time they regard you. And when you next meet, they may even mumble at you something that sounds like: "Origh'then?". More importantly, you will learn what their name is – and they might learn what yours is and that sort of thing really does break the barriers down.

Many older people nowadays think of the young as being another, quite separate, species. All of last summer for instance, there was a boy who mindlessly rode his noisy scooter, several times a day, up and down the street where I live. Whilst I ticked like an old meter about it, my friend asked. "Do you know *why* he does that?" I spat that I really had no twatting idea. "It's because it's his job." she replied. I thought about this and was suddenly catapulted back to a time at the frayed end of the 1960s when I was about his age. Noise? I made it. Stupid clothes? I wore them. Hair? All over my face. When I opened my mouth I was cocky, sloppily spoken and ignorant. When I was quiet, I was sullen and brooding. My very appearance had many of my elders incandescent with rage. Being a youth was *my* job back then and I worked very hard at it indeed.

In Wivenhoe, which still retains the basic framework of a community, it's still possible, with a bit of effort, to re-build some sort of flimsy bridge across the generational Grand Canyon that I've just described. In bigger towns, where the high streets are full of pubs guarded by bouncers, and herds of drunk young people queue outside for action – however that might be defined – it's much more difficult to see what can be done about the general disorder. Apart, of course, from yet more robust policing.

Over a century ago, on certain bank holidays, Brightlingsea youths would arrive in force by rail at Wivenhoe Station on the old 'Crab and Winkle' line in order to fight the home team. These punch-ups were no mean thing. Old archive reports detail incidences of pitched battles with stone throwing and mass brawling between the gangs. This combat might carry on sporadically over the course of an entire afternoon, until the police – or sometimes, the military police – came out to deal with it. The far more robust policing of the late-Victorian period was also augmented by an equally robust judicial system. Cases were usually fast-tracked within a day or two and often resolved – as mentioned earlier – by the birching or gaoling of the miscreants.

Yet, despite the why-oh-whyings of the concerned classes, in every sub-generation it seems, are instances of apparently normal young men just being irredeemably horrible little bastards: brawling, burgling, taking and selling drugs, drinking, breaking things, hurting people and generally being cruel and intimidating. One slight difference nowadays – in comparison to my own youth anyway – is that when I was young, many of our elders had done some sort of military service and had therefore been trained in the manly arts of self-defence or boxing. Unlike most of today's pudgy forty-somethings, they were wiry, relatively fit and crucially, they could still run. They also had, pretty much, carte blanche to exact retribution as they wished. For a teenager, to have a fit teacher or somebody else's tough dad bearing down on you at speed, was a thing to be reckoned with. They could and often did whack you. And if you told your own parents what had happened – as the old cliché runs – *they* whacked you too. The police in those days were also still allowed to shout at you, throw you against walls, hit you and find things upon your person, which, in a few cases, you hadn't even put there.

Being young was ever fraught with violence and fear, though probably not quite as much as during the two world wars, when of course, our government used to organise it all for us. Even in the late '60s and early '70s when I was in my own maytime, long-haired striplings such as myself spent much of our time hanging around the streets or, sometimes, pelting down them, pursued by first edition skinheads, intent upon hospitalising us. In fact, I once received a fairly comprehensive beating in a posh suburb of London in broad daylight just because of the way I was dressed.

As for alcohol: it was, in my youth, relatively expensive compared to today, harder to obtain and generally weaker. The pubs were fuller too. This was possibly because the licensing hours were fewer and you had to pack any drinking into time limits set, for the good of the nation, during the Great War. Pubs back then opened rather later, they closed earlier and were shut for most of the after-noon – except for Sundays, when they were shut for most of the day. Every tinpot convenience store and supermarket did *not* sell alcohol. You usually had to go to the off-licence shop to get it and even then, you'd have to deal with a, frankly, suspicious proprietor. Your drink-ing apprenticeship, therefore, had to be conducted under the stew-arding gaze of – if not your dad – men cast in a similar mould. In this way, some sort of drinking-etiquette was passed down from one's elders to their heirs.

This is not to say that there were never any general piss-ups, punch-ups or any of the myriad miseries and unpleasantness atten-dant upon them. There were always such things and they were every bit as foul as they are now. But people, young people, didn't have the opportunity, the money or the inclination to get *as* drunk – or as *frequently* drunk – as they do nowadays. Nor were they callous-ly encouraged to do so by a prevailing TV Yoof culture, supported by a ruthlessly adventurist drinks industry. Oh, and generally, you got into fearful trouble with *everyone*, if you produced a knife during the course of a disagreement.

Drunk, drugged, straight or sober though, today's young people can at times be bloody infuriating. They sit around in bracingly expensive, astoundingly ugly sports clothes, swear constantly and spend much of their time bawling a strange language at each other. Some of this I have learned to understand. For instance: "Shalaytorsdazza-yeah?" roughly translated, means: "Ah Darren. Perhaps we may possibly rendezvous on some future occasion? Goodbye then." Nearly everything that young people say these days, is a *question?* Such questions often have the word, "like" arbi-trarily inserted within them? And the music that they – like – *listen* to? Yeah? It often sounds rather like two mental patients arguing with each other, whilst putting up a shed? These, mind you, are just the English Lit students from the nearby university, who probably feel a desperate need to blend in. And it is *their* job to annoy *you*, now. Do not begrudge them such honest and timeless work.

As for the rest of Da Yoof – as we call them round these parts: the slit-mouthed hoodies, the teenage pram-faces and the smart-casual gangs of tattooed bruisers lurching and fighting around our town centres. I'd guess that they, too, are afraid of not blending in. But oh, they *do* blend in. They blend in to a stained tapestry of

English history which stretches all the way back to Romano-Celtic times, through murderous medieval football matches, through the gin-blitzed mob of the 18th century, right up to the Victorian razor gangs, 1920s mashers and all of yesteryear's teds, mods, rockers and punks. In conclusion, therefore, if Wivenhoe's Yoof really *aren't* any more stupid, violent, or inherently worse than any of their immediate predecessors were, the evidence seems to be that they're probably quite a bit drunker – and seemingly, quite a lot more of the time. Now, whose fault is *that*? Bring back the birch? Well, I agree. It's a lovely tree and planting a few might – like – foster their appreciation of the environment? Yeah? Wick-ed!

Chapter 9

Stroll On

Colchester is hugely historical. All the tourist literature will tell you so. Before we get into this, I'll walk you through a bit of my own history here. Let's ramble west up the High Street and wander round the corner. Here is North Hill. When you stand at the top, walking slowly downhill on the right hand side, beyond that sprawl, you'll still see distant green fields, spreading northwards to High Woods and beyond, to the old Severalls Hospital. Now pause by St Peter's stately old church with its distinctive clock sticking out at right angles to the tower. This church, in one form or another, was here before even the Normans arrived. And it was outside this very church, when I was in my mid-twenties, that a former long-term girlfriend of mine, by then with another chap, told me that she was going to have his baby. If I'd nurtured any small notion that we'd ever get back together again, it was here that I realised the game really was up. All my last hopes drank up and went home. This was the crushed out dog-end of my youth. Thatcher was in power, the Russians would soon roll into Afghanistan, punk rock was dead and my girl had gone. Adulthood began for me here.

A few yards down the hill, for many years, I also worked as a part-time kitchen porter in the Bistro at Number 9. One busy Christmas lunchtime, I and my fellow kitchen-porter Herbie, along with the restaurant's owner, Janet Brightmore – in all her antipodean loveliness – stood in the grey December drizzle, loading sacks of potatoes into a van. The potatoes, delivered by mistake, were found to be far too small for roasting and consequently, were being sent back to Jackson's warehouse in Osborne Street. Janet said she'd wired-up the bags, readying them for their return. This was all it took. Herbie and I were already hyped-up and in fine sea-sonal spirit. It was what we did. "Wired up? Electric potatoes?" we parroted at her. We stared at each other spiral-eyed, exploring all the possibilities again, before bursting into laughter. Still laughing, we each took a half cwt bag and struggled up the hill to where the Jackson's van was parked. In a robot voice, Herbie repeated:

"Electric potatoes!" And I burst out laughing again. An exasperated Janet finally slammed her bag down on the kerb, yelling: "Right! – That-Is-Ab-so-lutely E-Nough!" Her potato sack burst open. Hundreds of tiny potatoes began rolling down the hill, into the gutters and under the wheels of the lunchtime traffic. Herbie and I were now in hysterics, leaning against the van shrieking with laughter. The van driver was poker-faced and standing there completely nonplussed. Janet punched me on the shoulder, pushed Herbie and shouted at us in her Australian accent, "Don't just stand there. Gid aafter them!" Herbie and I, still shrieking with laughter, ran around on the hill chasing the potatoes, throwing them into apron pockets and dodging cars, till we'd got most of them back. Walking back down the hill later, with the two of us in tow and sniggering, Janet brushed her hands on her apron, suppressed a tight smile, and said: "God *knows* what that delivery driver made of it all. He must have thought he'd walked into a madhouse." It was fantastically funny and I can rarely walk down North Hill in winter without remembering that incident.

Further down North Hill, was Evans the Ironmonger. The shop had wooden floors and smelt of soap, paraffin and all sorts of wonderful things. Here's where I was sent from the Bistro for scourers, cleaning stuff, buckets and all sorts. Whatever you wanted, Evans nearly always had it. The men and women who worked there wore *Open All Hours* shop-coats and were knowledgeable and incredibly helpful. Evans, which had been there for 150 years or more, was a proper old-fashioned hardware shop. One day in the 1980s it closed. End of story. Market forces and all that It's a restaurant now. I've never been in there.

Just over the road was the surgery of Mr. York and Mr. Murphy, perfectly good NHS dentists. Mr. Murphy, when I was still a broke kitchen porter, once fought a Thatcher-era dental tribunal on my behalf, to make a case for me getting my teeth fixed on the NHS, which, years later, when they were bad enough, he eventually did. A few years later, out of gratitude to him, I dedicated one of my poetry collections to him. Up on the same side of North Hill, next to the Peveril Hotel and opposite the Bistro restaurant, was the Gilberd School. Many years before that, the old red-brick building had been part of the old Colchester County High School for Girls. It's the Sixth Form College now. Working beside me in the Bistro kitchen during the 1970s, was a feisty History of Art post-graduate of about my own age. She was called Nicky. I'm still friends with her. She's head of an art department over the road, now.

Many of my fellow restaurant staff at that time were just bohemian kids running around together, going out with each other, living out of each other's pockets, partying, seeing bands at the University and, sometimes, even singing with them. *We* were Colchester's youth back then and Colchester belonged to us. We lived in flats and bedsits off the Maldon Road or across town on East Hill. We were poor ragamuffins, scraping by in make-do jobs. We had no idea where we'd all end up. Thirty-odd years down the line, it's surprising for me to find that many of us still live in the area. A few of us became teachers, lecturers, writers or artists. One of the waitresses went back to college, took her law exams and became a solicitor. Another is now the landlady of a Wivenhoe B&B – a very classy one at that. One of my fellow former porters now runs a top-notch Colchester hairdresser's. The woman who prepped the vegetables eventually became a successful restaurateur herself. A faded colour snapshot of us all – porters, waitresses and cooks – standing outside the Bistro in our stripey aprons one sunny spring morning in late 1970s, does not reveal anything about our possible futures.

In the picture, most of us look scruffy, broke and cheerful. At the time, you probably wouldn't have placed a bet on us as the team-most-likely-to. Individually, most of us eventually, ended up doing something useful.

Sometimes, if the lunchtime tips had been good, a few of us would go in late afternoon to Jacklin's restaurant for posh tea and toast. The restaurant, which was just around the corner in the High Street, was situated above Mr. Jacklin's tobacconist shop. It was one of Colchester's great old shops. Sitting in the upstairs tearoom was like a trip back in time to the respectable 1930s. The waitresses wore black dresses and white aprons. The tablecloths were linen. Tea was served in pots. Toast was golden. The place was oak-panelled, with big picture windows looking down upon the High Street. And there among the genteel middle-aged women of Colchester, who'd been shopping in Williams & Griffin, we sat too, drinking our tea and gossiping before trailing home to our rented flats, shared houses and bedsits. And I'd walk home down the High Street to East Hill, usually stopping to gaze in the window of Mann's Music shop. Here's a little bit of Colchester history for you, then:

All things considered, the year 1854 was an eventful one. Britain declared war on Russia in the spring. In autumn, Florence Nightingale left for the Crimea with 38 nurses. Charles Dickens wrote and serialised his novel, Hard Times. *Cholera, meanwhile, had broken out in London killing 10,000 people. And Frederick Mann opened his first music shop in St. John's Street, Colchester. Mann's Music at 156 years old, is not just the oldest music shop in Colchester, it's thought to be the oldest in the country to have been under continuous ownership. Frederick Mann, whose local ancestry can be traced back to a 17th century weaver, manufactured and sold harmoniums − a kind of treadle-powered chapel organ. He then began selling pianos, violins, and sheet music.*

There were a couple of relocations before the Mann family finally settled at their present 123 High Street premises. That was 118 years ago. And I've probably been shuffling in there for the last 36 of them − for guitars, harmonicas, picks, strings, straps and other musical widgets. A music shop must swing with the times − a thing which Mann's seems to have managed well. When Frederick Mann died in 1894, he was succeeded by his sons and, for a few years, the shop went under the name of Mann Brothers. In the early years of 20th century, the technology shifted up a key, when the first recorded music arrived in the form of the Edison Bell wax cylinder, which Mann Brothers began to sell. Gramophones soon followed, with 78 rpm shellac records and later, mass-produced wireless sets. By 1937, only one of the Mann brothers, Robert, was running the shop. Upon his death in 1949, his son Sidney took over and by the late 1950s, when Sidney's son David took up the baton, the shop was selling tape-recorders, radiograms and vinyl long players.

A decade or so earlier, Sidney had married Joan Davies, a girl from a shop just down the High Street, whose family sold weighing scales. When World War II intervened − whilst Sydney did his bit for the RAF in Africa and Germany − Joan ran the shop single-handedly until his return. "She went from selling one type of scales to another?" I asked Tim Mann, the shop's current managing director. The penny dropped and he laughed: "I hadn't thought of that." His grandfather regularly wrote home to Joan though and the correspondence, which the family still has in its possession, is rather moving to read, says Tim.

Tim Mann took over from his dad, David, in 1997, having, like his father before him, worked in the shop since he was a teenager. He is now the fifth generation of the Mann family to have done so. When I later talked to his father, David Mann remembered the gramophones, their needles and the individual auditioning booths, in which his customers used to listen to records before they bought them. *"Singles cost six shillings and eightpence when I first started buy-ing them."* I told him. *"I think they were three and fourpence when I started."* he replied.

Underneath an obvious love of music though, I noted a certain steely busi-ness sense in both father and son. *They know how to bend with the capricious wind of progress. When asked about Internet sales, I was surprised when Mr. Mann Senior calculated that 30 to 40 percent of their sales are now conducted online. A constant in the Mann business method seems to have been the ability to keep up with such unpredictable trends.*

And yet, there are certain long-term staples at Mann's Music. They stock a huge range of sheet music and songbooks, for instance. The golden age of music publishing preceded even the gramophone and yet sales are still bearing up remarkably well. *"It's the foundation of our business,"* stated Mr. Mann Junior. Downstairs, Julie, the shop's elegant sheet-music department manager told me that she can't believe how well Abba songbooks are selling at the moment. *"And Leonard Cohen collections – in the wake of Hallelujah's recent chart success?"* I asked. She nodded and smiled. Julie has been at Mann's Music for 17 years, since she completed her education. *"What about the Beatles?"* I asked her. A cus-tomer at the counter gestured at a shelf-full of Beatles songbooks and interjects: *"They'll never die, will they?"* The shop also still sells traditional and orches-tral instruments and all their accoutrements. In fact, you can buy anything here – from a tin whistle for a few pounds, to a baby-grand piano for about £6,000.

Not that Mann's doesn't also keep up with the baffling and ever-shifting rock trends. Much as the TV talent judge Peter Waterman might hate it, rackety Indie guitar music is currently all the rage again and Mann's is suitably armoured to supply the kit for it. Keyboard sales are at somewhat of a plateau, but, said Tim, guitar sales are holding up well. Indeed, I found that Alex, the young chap in charge of them, knew all about Hofners – the vintage German guitars beloved of musical recidivists like me. He barely looked old enough. He even gave me the name of a local specialist who could service mine, a much-abused Hofner V3 made in 1960 complete with toast-rack pick-ups and tremo-lo arm. That's only 106 years younger than the music emporium that Frederick Mann of Colchester founded in 1854.

Before I went into Mann's Music to find out about their histo-ry for an article I was researching for the *East Anglian Daily Times*, I probably hadn't even given it too much thought. But Colchester is full of shop doorways and peculiar little corners which each new generation, drunk on their own youth and lost in their own dramas, never think of as anything other than a place to snog in, shelter from the rain, fight outside of or, occasionally, throw-up over. Until one day later in life, upon starting a business of their own, as Mr. Mann and Mr. Jacklin, the tobacconist, once did, some of them begin to realise that the bricks of the town are far older than they are. And Colchester High Street, being roughly in the same place as its Roman counterpart once stood, has been witnessing such enlightenment now for two thousand years or more.

In May of 1979, while I was still working in the kitchen at 9 North Hill, the roofers arrived to do some repairs. One afternoon, as I was finishing my shift, they invited me to climb up the ladder and have a look around on the roof. The building must have been at least three, or maybe four hundred years old. From there, I could see across many of the other old roofs and get a genuine sense of Colchester's antiquity. I could see the tops of trees that I'd never noticed before. The limeade haze of early summer had spread itself out across the town's northern outskirts. Above me was the blue sky. Below me was the sound of the afternoon traffic. I was standing in the sunlight on the roof of a building. The building was on a hill at the top of an old Essex market town. I looked down, as its original builders must once have done, at the lay of the land. It was a peculiar sensation. Then Simon, the head roofer, said, "Have a look at this, Martin." He presented me with a rusty old spur that they'd found in the roof valley trough that morning. I turned the object over in my hands. How the hell had it got there? A horseman's spur? Maybe some 18th century drunks had done the classic thing of throwing a mate's boot up onto a roof after a session on the ale. Maybe a Civil War defender, up there watching the northern approaches, had been forced to get down in a hurry and had ripped the spur off in his haste, before cursing and scurrying down the wooden ladder. Perhaps some tricorn-hatted market lad had just found it in the street one morning and slung it up there. One thing was certain – and Simon knew a little about such things – it was very old and it had been up there for a long time. It had lain up there since before radios, before cars, before television, before Penicillin, before electric lights and before almost everything invented which we live with and take for granted now. Somebody – who had long ago turned to dust – had left behind or lobbed a spur up on the roof of number 9 North Hill. History is exactly this for me. I know very little, for instance, about the deeper causes of the

English Civil War. But an old spur turned up in a roof valley by some long-haired 1970s Essex roofers? *That*, I could marvel at and understand. Come closer now...

Chapter 10

The Rich Karaoke Of History

I'm no kind of historian, but I'm very interested in the past and have become even more so since writing for the East Anglian Daily Times. When researching a particular subject, I have often found a more fascinating story underneath the one which I had initially thought I was writing. Here follow five stories to do with Colchester's past, which illustrate this very well.

1. Mediaeval Colchester

I've lately been absorbed in a new book called *Mediaeval Colchester's Lost Landmarks*. Well, these days, it's the kind of guy I am. I now fall upon such items with the sort of enthusiasm that I might, three decades ago, have reserved for say, a new David Bowie album. Colchester is rich in history – so rich in fact, that it's easy to miss great chunks of it out. The problem that Colchester has with its historical oeuvre is the same problem that certain old rock-stars have. People only want to hear the greatest hits, which in this town's case are Roman Colchester and the English Civil War. Historically speaking, they've become a sort of karaoke, which the heritage business encourages everyone to sing along with, ignoring in the process a great swathe of equally important material.

John Ashdown-Hill, the author of the book, sets out his stall in the first few paragraphs of his introduction. His point, which is a very fair one, is that there's a whole five hundred years' worth of Colchester's history that we hardly ever hear about. The back cover of the book, unknowingly, hints at part of the story. For here, in the foreground, is the beautiful carved mediaeval portal of the Red Lion pub – once Howard's Place. Yet, just in the background, under the beamed arch by the hotel entrance, is all the modern detritus – the Coke cans and chip-wrappers – of a Saturday night on the town. A juxtaposition of venerable craftsmanship versus modern throwaway culture? Think again. According to our historian, our forbears were no slouches when it came to litter and general pollution.

One big problem in mediaeval Colchester was the human dunghill. Before the invention of modern sanitation, dunghills sprang up anywhere and everywhere. You found them in East Stockwell Street, by the side of the Priory, and even in the High Street, in front of the Moot Hall. Not only that, but a local butcher, one Robert Cok, was in the habit of emptying his chamber pots out over an already less-than-fragrant East Stockwell Street. You now have to factor in the added delights of poultry, horses and of course, various pigs wandering around the town centre. Funny old place, the past – ingenious architecture and sub-Glastonbury toilet facilities.

Yet it wasn't all filth and ordure. Outside the old walled town, the ground sloped away in all directions, revealing a vista of woodland, fields and water meadows. Inside the walls were many green spaces, wells, orchards, pleasant gardens and trees. And as well as St. John's Abbey, St. Botolph's Priory and the Franciscan Friary, there were also eight parish churches. Colchester's population doubled during the Middle Ages, from an estimated two-and-a-half-thousand, to almost six-thousand souls. At one point it was the eighth largest provincial town in England and probably a very lively prospect on a feast day, or an evening out. The mediaeval mindset may have been very different to our own; the appetites, however, were broadly similar.

After a few ales, therefore, what better than to catch the bear baiting in Vineyard Street – then called Bere Street. This was an outdoor pursuit, requiring only a simple bear-stake to tether the hapless creature to while a pack of fierce dogs attacked it. The bear didn't always get killed though. A bear – imported from the continent because of domestic shortages – was an expensive commodity. They pulled him out after they reckoned he'd had enough, so that he could recover from his wounds and fight again. Other entertainments consisted of the taverns, the gallows, the pillory and of course the brothels, which were seen as a necessary evil, to prevent good men from turning to homosexuality. Most brothels, again, were in the Bere Street vicinity and not far from the scenes of drunken carousing known to modern-day revellers. Amazing how certain urban areas have a habit of echoing their own history isn't it? With some places it's almost as if licentious behaviour is imprinted in the very stones.

Though it is stone, or the acute shortage of it in this area, which is probably the chief reason why there's so little of mediaeval Colchester left. Stone was re-cycled time and time again. In one account here, for instance, a chap is fined for pinching bits of the town walls for underpinning his new houses. Another man is pulled up for selling six barrow loads of stone to a Frenchman. The bulk of Mr. Ashdown-Hill's book, however, does not dwell on the petty crime, social ills or corporeal excesses of the townspeople – fascinating as they may be. The book also contains a thorough and lovingly researched look at Colchester's religious houses, hospitals and its many other buildings.

Much of that mediaeval town, though by no means all of it, has now disappeared. If you want to see the vestiges of lost Colchester, you only have to squint your eyes and look a little harder, as the author has done. Alternatively, following his mediaeval map you could turn right at Frere Street (top of East Hill) go down South Street (Queen Street) and turn right again into Bere Street, (Vineyard Street) where the poor folk, the prostitutes and bear-baiters used to meet. It's just after the Norman Conquest, carry on past the Black Death and stop just before the Reformation. You can't miss it.

2. God Comes Back To Maidenburgh Street

The day they took possession of it, priest and worshippers had gathered on the small green in nearby St. Helens Lane. It was the first religious service that the building had witnessed in 461 years. During this time, among many other things, St. Helen's Chapel had been a private house, a shop and a workshop. When the small congregation entered and began to sing, "It sounded as if the walls themselves were singing back at us, asking us: 'Where have you been all this time?'"

It is very hard – even for a benighted heathen like myself – not to be moved by Father Alexander Haig's account of how in the year 2000, the Orthodox Church came back to the chapel in Maidenburgh Street, Colchester. The emotion is in his voice and in his eyes while he tells this story.

St. Helen, or St. Helena as many call her, was mother of Constantine the Great and of course, Patron Saint of Colchester. Depending upon which sources you believe, she was born nearby in

Colchester Castle, which was then her father, King Coel's castle. She is said to have built the chapel for her own worship. According to history though, she was actually born in Asia Minor – modern-day Turkey. Here religious doctrine, local legend and blurred historical accounts all conspire together to make what Hollywood film-makers would call 'a reality soup'.

One thing is for certain though. St. Helen's Chapel is very, very old. Nobody knows exactly how old, but it was here before the Normans arrived and even then its restoration was on their To Do list. Appearances can be deceptive. The chapel's walls, three of which are on the foundations of the ancient Roman Theatre, have seen much rebuilding over the centuries. The exterior, in a town rich in other historical treasures, is a rather unspectacular Victorian one. It is the interior that is so interesting. The luminous red-golds of the saintly icons, that line the chapel's walls – along with the candles, which quietly hiss and sputter during my visit – combine to make the little church far more atmospheric than many much grander places of worship.

Father Haig does his erudite best to crash-course me through the basic history of Orthodox Christianity, which is fascinating. Eastern Orthodoxy was the earliest form of Christianity. Catholicism is a stripling by comparison. A schism occurred between Eastern Christianity (Greek) and its rival Roman Catholicism (Latin) in the 11th century. The emergent Catholic Church, in turn, experienced its own dissenters a few centuries later and so Protestantism was born. Father Haig himself was an Anglican priest for three decades, but converted to Orthodox in the mid 1990s. The matter of women vicars, he says, was the issue which prompted his decision. Looking around St. Helen's now and absorbing something of its overwhelming mystique, I can partly sympathise with this. If you'd been brought up with a theological package – one rich in ritual and reverence – and then woken one day to find that your place of worship was now full of people playing drum kits, blasting saxophones and guitars and happily clapping along, all conducted by someone a bit like Dawn French in her *Vicar of Dibley* role, might you not yearn for a return to an older, weightier, wholemeal faith – one with no additives and nowt-taken-out, so to speak? The matter is obviously more complex than this but it is the simplest explanation that a theological chowderhead such as I can muster.

Father Haig's flock comprises Greeks, Greek-Cypriots, Bulgarians, Serbs, Arab-Christians and others. There may be between thirty and fifty worshippers attending any one service. One feature of an Orthodox service is that all music is chanted or sung. The Orthodox faith believes that the voice comes from the soul, whereas musical instruments are of the earth. Similarly, the Sanctuary of the church, which represents heaven, is curtained off from the Nave, the area where the congregation pray. The Sanctuary may be observed when the curtains are opened but only the priest has access to this area. "It is," adds Father Haig, using an Olympian analogy, "as if life were a race, and this, were the stadium." Here he points at the many icons of the saints. "And these, are our spectators who cheer us on, should we tire or falter."

Perhaps it is the sheer antiquity of St. Helen's Chapel, or maybe it's something to do with the candles, the icons and the quiet measured tone of the priest's voice. But time seems to dissolve while I listen to him and I suddenly find that an hour has slipped by in what seems like five minutes. As I walk out dazed into the cold drizzle of Maidenburgh Street, I pause to look back down the hill and north to the distant fields on the outskirts of town. Well over a thousand years ago, when the Riverside Estate to the east was still marsh and water meadows, a St. Helen's Chapel, in some form or other, existed here. At the top of Maidenburgh Street, the High Street bustles moodily about its midweek business. Two minutes walk away, nestling in quiet side streets, is this ancient, holy building that has somehow fallen back into the hands of the very faith that created it. St. Helen's Chapel is Number 2 on Colchester's Heritage Trail. It's also on a rather older, more venerable trail – one which leads all the way back to Antioch.

3. Saxons versus Romans

Scarcely a week goes by in Colchester it seems, without a new Roman find being unearthed. Not that this affects me much, either way. I'm inured to it. The town has an embarrassment of archaeological riches. We've got the castle, a theatre, numerous bits of old wall and recently discovered, the only example of a Roman circus in the whole country. Ever since I was a piping-voiced, whey-faced boy, Colcestrians have been turning up Roman helmets in their gardens, and finding lead coffins made for dead Roman children under their kitchen extensions. Building contractors and pipe-layers must by now have learned to dread working in central Colchester, because the minute they swing the first pickaxe, it bites into a Minervan statue or a fluted column and everything has to stop for ages while the archaeologists go in.

I once used to know some archaeologists. Thanks to popular TV programmes such as *Time Team*, people nowadays have a rough idea of what it is that they do all day. Back in the mid-1970s however, they were mostly, unsung heroes. In those days my local was a pub on East Hill, The Ship. After work, the young 'diggers' used to come, aching and muddy from their sites, into the public bar. They were usually scruffy, hairy, prematurely bearded, fond of ale and with a penchant for listening to the more difficult prog-rock bands. I found that many of the male archaeologists were also like that. In fact, one of them was quite the worst bar billiards player I'd ever seen, managing, habitually, to knock over all the mushrooms on the table in one disastrous shot. Another was obsessed mainly with pinball – The Ship had a particularly fiendish pinball machine. A third digger was an ex-American GI, who, having studied archaeology as part of his civilian rehabilitation, had opted to come here because he'd "Gotten kinda bored with diggin' up dead Injuns," and had decided that digging up dead Romans was far more interesting. We made friends with the diggers. Like us, they were mostly in their early twenties and they occasionally told us curious local lads what it was that they did. They said that they spent a lot of time carefully washing potsherds and even more time on their hands and knees learning how to use a trowel gingerly. Mostly, they told us, it was a race against time. If a new building or shopping precinct was going up, for instance, they often only had a few weeks stay-of-execution to go in and root around before the new concrete was poured in and any potential door open to the past was slammed shut for another century or so.

It was explained to us that Colchester's Roman High Street was roughly where our modern one is today. Underneath this, at various points, existed a burnt layer of soil where, in AD 61, a furious Boudicca had burnt the cakes – and everything else – after the

Romans, who'd stolen her lands, whipped her and then publicly brutalised her two twelve year-old girls. It's stirring stuff and it's somehow typical of our underdog sympathies that it is Boudicca who is remembered rather than Suetonius Paulinus, her Roman destroyer.

Roman Colchester was an important town for its time and since the Romans were here for several hundred years they left rather a lot of stuff lying around. In fact as I stumble across the High Street between say, Mann's Music and the HSBC bank, I do periodically, wonder what's lying underneath the pavements. Only periodically, mind you. The thing is, I've never really liked the Romans much. They had silly haircuts, they wore dresses on their days off and they all went to the bathroom together. They were expansionist bullies and invented a system of government that, to this day, is still making epic cock-ups all over the world. Okay, they were good builders – but what else have they ever done for us – apart from leaving us the ceiling rose? This is a true story: It used to be an actual rose once, which they hung above the dinner table because they believed it promoted the telling of truth; a thing, incidentally, which I've often found is not necessarily the best idea at the dinner table. Their rose, though, eventually became a decorative plaster rose and finally, morphed into that round white plastic widget that your light-flex hangs from today. Fascinating, hey? Let's move on.

I prefer the Saxons, myself. Unreconstructed ruralists, they built their houses with biodegradable materials, had rock star haircuts, made great jewellery and wore excellent trousers. When the Saxons hit a place, after a while – like most good Englishmen still do today – they calmed down a bit, married a local girl and kept animals. And what's wrong with that? We hardly ever hear of Saxon Colchester, though. Why? Well, they weren't the supreme egotists that Romans seemed to be and they didn't have the corresponding compulsion to leave their signatures everywhere. If we were to leave the amount of junk around now that the Romans did, Westminster would be onto us like ferrets, telling us to clear it all up and waffling on about sustainability. The Saxons, though, compared their lifespan to the flight of a sparrow, which having flown out of the stormy night, came momentarily into the warmth and noise of a feasting-hall before flying back out into the cold darkness. Now there's a poetic philosophy. Try selling it to an archaeologist though.

4. Return of the Universal Soldier

"There are dead Crimean War soldiers, buried under there." says George, pointing to a piece of greensward behind the Officers Club tennis courts. George, a spry and genial octogenarian has been the car park attendant at the pinnacled 15th century St. John's Abbey Gatehouse for the past 14 years. He's also a fund of information. He points in the direction of Colchester's old Cavalry Barracks, built in 1861 and asks me if I know how many horses were stabled there during the Great War. Over 2,000 of them at one point, he tells me. The soldiers slept in rooms above the stables. Horses, you see, give off quite a lot of heat – which would have helped keep the cavalrymen's billets warm. When the cavalry was needed for France, said George, they took the horses down to nearby St. Botolph's Station, where they were entrained and taken by cattle-truck to the coast. Many of them, horses and men, would never return, having perished in the mud of Flanders. Of the buried Crimean War soldiers, he said that English Heritage knew about them and that the area was sacred ground. George, a former Coldstream Guardsman returned home from his own war on the troopship SS Empire Windrush – the same ship which later brought the first Jamaican migrant workers to Britain in 1948.

I met George quite by chance. I'd decided to go in search of the old Colchester Garrison. The streets of this town have echoed to the tread of soldiers' feet for almost two thousand years now. A major barracks existed here in Napoleonic times. In the late 18th century, the soldiers were billeted in local homes and inns. But as more and more of them arrived, it became an increasingly uncomfortable arrangement. After fierce petitioning from the townsfolk, the troops – artillery, cavalry and infantry were newly garrisoned in the area now known as New Town. The barracks were bounded by Wimpole Road to the west and Port Lane to the east. By 1800, when Edward Jenner himself – the discoverer of the smallpox vaccine – arrived to inoculate an entire regiment against the disease, Colchester, with its population of around 11,000, found itself with another town bolt-ed onto its flank. Not that this was an entirely bad thing, for it must have generated a certain amount of trade. Then, too, as has happened ever since, some of the soldiers appear to have settled down with local girls. Incredibly, in 1856, there were also 10,000 German troops – recruited for use in the Crimean War, stationed here. At first, they and their 12-man huts were fenced in, for fear of hostility from townsmen. In fact, they were rather popular in the town and the new wooden Garrison Church hosted a large number of Anglo-German marriages shortly afterwards. Over the decades not all of the soldiers sent here were lucky enough to get huts, however. Many lived under canvas. They drilled on Abbey Fields, Middlewick Range, or elsewhere, until marching-out time came, when they had to leave their sweethearts, children and their memories behind them.

The relationship between town and garrison has not been without a certain friction over the years. From a military family myself, in my youth, I commonly heard the word 'squaddy' used in certain town pubs – and used in some contempt too. Though as Rudyard Kipling wrote: "It's Tommy this and Tommy that and 'Chuck him out, the brute.' / But it's 'saviour of his country' when the guns begin to shoot." Colchester is still one of Britain's biggest garrison towns and there's a strong affection for the army here too.

Cycling through the old garrison now with its stern, imposing-looking Victorian buildings, I'm reminded of the Army bases of my childhood. It's not so much a look – more of a *feel*. They could just as easily be in Aldershot, Chester or Catterick. They seem in their way, to still be standing at attention somehow – as if full of the ghosts of old RSMs awaiting the arrival of yet another regiment. Round in pretty St. John's Green, in the shadow of the Gatehouse, George, the former guardsman is on duty in his sentry box, a small, cosy shed. George's tame robin is pecking at a slice of bread nearby. Through the Gatehouse archway, which has witnessed the numberless boots and hooves of the centuries pass beneath it, comes a smartish car. A ruddy-faced young man is at the wheel. He's possibly an army officer. He looks a little like Prince William. He addresses George crisply, with one word: "Luncheon?" George points at the Officers Club and politely takes care of the matter.

Wheeling towards Port Lane, down tree-lined Harsnett Road, which for me, is one of Colchester's most elegant suburban streets, it occurs to me that two centuries ago, in the run-up to Waterloo, this quiet area would have been full of tents, horses, gun carriages and sergeants yelling at soldiers. Men who had fought all over Europe knew this ground – and would continue to do so for many years to come. The Universal Soldier knows Colchester rather well.

5. St. Botolph's Priory – Fur Coat and No Knickers

St. Botolph's Priory needs a bit of a spruce-up. It's long overdue of course. In heritage industry terms, St. Botolph's, in all its shattered grandeur, is Colchester's most neglected old lady. Founded circa 1103, only decades after the Norman Conquest, it was England's first Augustinian priory and in 1116 was recognised as such by Pope Pascal II. The problem was that it had no major 'sponsor' – no aristocrat or royal was bankrolling it. Despite its nominal seniority, therefore, compared to later but wealthier priories, St. Botolph's was not particularly well-heeled. This, as northerners used to say, was a fur-coat-and-no-knickers situation, similar in fact, to the one in which the monument finds itself now.

St. Botolph's, like so many religious houses, fell into decline after Henry the Eighth's row with the Church of Rome in 1536. In the mid-seventeenth century, it sustained severe damage during the Siege of Colchester. Over the ensuing centuries, rather like our regional rail network, the place changed owners several times again, though, seemingly, without the re-branding, the paint jobs or the regular weekend 'improvements'.

As a result, St. Botolph's Priory is a ruin, a beautiful ruin. Its entrance is tucked discreetly away in Priory Street, though one of the best views of it may be obtained from the platform at Colchester Town rail station. From there, peering over the red-brick wall you may get some idea of its proportions; not just what remains of it now, but what had once existed. It's attractively set too, with trees overlooking its northern flank and its floors long-reverted to a swathe of uneven greensward.

St. Botolph's chief problem as a heritage site and tourist attraction seems to be that it remains a favourite hangout of stunt-drinkers, drug addicts and sundry other no-goodniks. The poor, as the clergy are fond of saying, are always with us. Every town has them. Their faces, unshaven and unloved, have the complexion of weathered cider apples. Their eyes glint watchfully at strangers as they loll around mumbling and laughing gap-toothed among themselves. Periodically, one might get up and stagger over to another for a furtive exchange of goods or a slug on a bottle. Naturally, many members of the public find them intimidating. The authorities have recently recognised this fact and now acknowledge that the ruins of St. Botolph's deserve better. They want to make the place more attractive, perhaps even to stage open-air theatre productions there and to clear out the mendicants, the boozers and the druggies.

I find it interesting, though, that the perceived swarf of society should congregate in such a place. If you examine the psycho-geography of the matter, St. Botolph's is an ancient holy site, close to a railway station, a bus station and a gothic Victorian church – all of them in their own ways places of transit. At night, the area comes alive, with fast food eateries, nightclubs and taxis. Only a kebab's throw away from here, the young revellers arrive at weekends to kick the working week in the head and sometimes, each other. In mediaeval times, just outside the old town walls, this is where you'd find the poor, the bear-baiters and the brothels. It's a classic location – the lonely and the lost have always drifted here. You'll meet them lurching baseball-capped and grubby, dragging their squat dogs past Colchester Town station where the police will occasionally stop and search them. Oddly enough, after writing this piece, I found out that St. Botolph is the Patron Saint of itinerants.

But who are these itinerants – and where did they come from? How, in our still-wealthy modern society do they slip through the net, invisible and uncared for? A significant proportion of homeless men, if you should ever stop to speak to them, are former soldiers. Talk to one before he's shotgunned his second tin of super-lager and you may find that he was once in Kosovo or Iraq. He's the modern counterpart of the maimed, half-blind soldiers from Wellington's army who, upon return from Flanders or Spain cluttered England's squares and church steps in the years after Waterloo. He's seen the world. He didn't like it much. He didn't talk about it, because no one who hadn't been there could possibly understand what it had been like. And gradually, as he tumbled darkly through the tunnel, arguing on the way with all the people who might have helped him, he got lost. Finally, he found the company of all the others who stagger from booze shop to bench and back again. Move him on and, like pushing down a bubble in bit of wallpaper, he'll pop up somewhere else. Perhaps it'll be the St. Mary's churchyard or somewhere near Colchester Castle. But it will nearly always be somewhere ancient, the type of place, which for centuries people in straits have been inexplicably drawn to. No one ever chooses such a lifestyle as a career move. They just fall by gradual stages into ruin – much like St. Botolph's has done.

St. Botolph's, though, deserves and must get its thirsted-for makeover. Maybe a theatre company could take charge of it? Perhaps they could stage Beckett's perennially popular *Waiting For Godot*, a play about two tramps waiting for somebody, or something that never turns up? That would be suitably ironic wouldn't it: actors in the role of tramps, to replace the real ones? How very heritage industry that that would be.

Chapter 11

To The Sea...

It is claimed by some that if you include all its creeks and little islands, Essex has the biggest coastline in England. Whilst this may or may not be true, officially, at least, the county is credited with having the country's third biggest coastline. For many years, my uncle, a smallholder in landlocked Buckinghamshire, brought his family to Clacton for their annual summer holiday. Clacton and Walton, loved by the Victorian denizens of the old East End who gave both seaside towns a cheery zippiness. I get rather fed up with hearing certain fellow Essex residents running the places down.

Some call it 'Chavton' or 'Cracktown.' Yes, it has lowlife and of course you may see two wretches with homemade tattoos, speeding along the pavement engaged in some frantic argument about supply, demand and late-payment for god-knows-what. You'll also see morbidly obese scummy-mummies, bellowing coarsely at young children who are already displaying a glint of early-onset pathos in their deprived eyes. On a sunny morning, flabby young men with their shirts off may be observed lounging outside bars, laughing raucously and shot-gunning their first Stellas of the day. You'll see all of this – if you're looking for it. And I could probably name you at least fifty other places in the UK where you could view exactly the same tableaux, or worse.

Clacton deserves a better reputation than it has and at time of writing, I believe that it's actually on the way back up. It's a peculiarly English sort of thing, though, running places down. If you listen to all the negative stuff about Essex, you will learn that Frinton is snobbish and full of old people. It actually isn't. It's polite and charming, it has a great shopping street and many young families live there. As for Walton: Well, according to the same sources, Walton isn't what it used to be. And Harwich? Why would anyone go to Harwich? Or Jaywick? Crazy! Never even mention it.

But these places aren't just jokes to be tossed around in gastro-pubs by olive-scoffing wazzocks who should really know better. They're real towns, with real communties of people who like living there and they elect councils who are usually engaged in doing their very best to promote them. They have their own histories, monuments, characters, charms and pride. They also have the sea. The beautiful sea. Here, culled from my columns for the East Anglian Daily Times, are some of my own experiences.

1. Clacton

It's one of those silvery summer mornings that the Essex coast is so good at and I'm standing on Clacton Pier having what the Americans call 'a quality moment.' With the North Sea's heaving grey fleece behind me, I am looking back towards Clacton town, to the golden sweep of the beach and the white Victorian buildings on the land. I'm trying to see what its creator, Peter Bruff, envisaged all those years ago and I think I may have succeeded. Clacton-on-Sea was a great idea – a great idea that worked. You build a town on a barely used bit of coastline – the driest part of England – and you make it look a little bit like a *Happy Shopper* version of the south of France. You then put in a pier and some wedding cake hotels and – because the railways don't quite reach that far yet – you bring your trippers in by packet steamer. Peter Bruff, the visionary engineer who also built much of Walton, is often described nowadays as the Richard Branson of his time. In the 1870s, despite strident objections from Clacton's then rural council, he invested oodles of cash in the place, sorted out new roads and drains and began building as if there was no tomorrow.

Bruff had originally wanted Clacton to be more of an upmarket resort, like Frinton, but the railways, for whom he'd originally worked, got to the place first. Within a few years the day trippers were arriving in their eager thousands. Though, to Elsie and Horace from Bethnal Green or Bow, on a Whitsun works outing away from the match factory, Clacton must have seemed like heaven. As they stepped out onto the newly-improved pier they would have seen, very roughly, what can still be seen today: the azure sky, the golden sand and the green and white flashes of the trees and houses just above the promenade. Then, like pit ponies let up from the dark mines into the summer meadows, they would have yearned for it ever after.

Clacton, when it's sunny, as it is today, is a town that feels like it's bunked off for the day. In the pleasant avenues just outside the town centre, relaxed retirees in beige shorts and Hawaiian shirts are posting letters and clipping hedges. In the slightly down-at-heel town centre, pavements are crowded and the charity shops and early lunchtime cafes are busy. On the promenade, shirtless be-trainered men are already filling the seats outside the seafront bars to worship at the fountain of St. Ella – patron saint of misunderstandings. Sure it's cheap and cheerful – so what? You think you wouldn't hear the odd vulgarity in St. Tropez or Sienna, if you'd bothered to learn the language? The difference here is that your lunch only costs about six quid and the chemist immediately understands whatever it is that you've asked for.

The shame of it – in the run-up to a bank holiday – is that the pier upon which I'm standing is practically deserted. The sea-bleached boards echo to the tread of the few people amiably strolling around on them. But the *Jolly Roger* restaurant at the pier's end is open, serving perfect golden chips, fish, pies, and teas. The dodgems and gaming arcades are still closed, but the fortune-teller's doing a good business. My companion and I conclude that this place is – and I deliberately use a 1960s adjective here – 'smashing'. Three people that we didn't even know have said good morning to us, there was no charge to go on the pier and the view is brilliant. And yet there are hardly any punters. Why? It would be a great place for instance, to go for breakfast or even – as my companion rather keenly pointed out – to get married. You could have the reception in the restaurant and a dance band outside making as much racket as they wanted.

I ask myself why people would spend sixty grand on a beach hut at Southwold, or stand in a stupid airport queue at Stansted, when they could be doing this. Though, as I look at the peeling paintwork and the salt corrosion on surrounding metalwork, there's also a melancholy side to it. It's like one of those maltreated Spanish donkeys that the tabloids usually feature during the silly season – you want to ring in and adopt it. It's high time the old girl had a bit of a makeover.

2. Frinton

Frinton, it's claimed, was the last town in England to be attacked by the Luftwaffe. This is easy enough to believe. BBC documentary crew aside, Frinton is the last place that anyone would want to attack. Until one morning in 1944, that is, when Hermann Goering probably clapped his hand to his head, skipped over to his staff phone and gushed excitedly: "You'll never guess what, guys? We've only gone and forgotten Frinton. Ha ha – I know! Bonkers isn't it?

But hey, that's war. Oh, and remember to strafe those new Art Deco houses on the Walton side. That's right. How many? I dunno. About forty of them it says here. You can't miss 'em. They're bright white with loads of snazzy windows. Thanks. Byeee. No, you first. Oh alright then. Mwah! Love you, too!"

Luckily for Frinton, the Art Deco houses on its Walton side came out of the Luftwaffe's last raid unscathed. If you've never seen them, and you like that sort of thing, they're really worth a visit. Frinton is the site of the largest group of such houses in the country. They were built in the mid-1930s at a time when the country was still in the throes of a huge housing boom. Frinton though – ever an upmarket place – appears to have been the setting for a battle royal between two distinct schools of architecture. On one flank are the town's graceful Avenues, which are crammed with classic Tudorbethan mansions and an attendant flummery of gables and crenellations. These, for all their self-conscious English-retro are actually redolent of a Hollywood film set. Here, we can imagine, Frinton's famous colonels, admirals, surgeons and matrons retired to write their memoirs. According to local hearsay, however, there were also quite a few celebrities of the day – mainly showbiz types. Celebrities of the 1920s and '30s though, weren't quite as gauche as their modern counterparts. They tended not to tattoo their bottoms, punch photographers or smoke crack whilst a documentary crew filmed them. Instead they favoured breakfasting late in bed, taking bubble baths and then donning tweeds and going inland for a bit of shooting. The result of this is that nobody now remembers who most of them were, though Douglas Fairbanks (Sr.) was reportedly one of them. Far from being the royalty-lite that our celebs are today, showbiz folk then were often regarded as somewhat declassé by the true aristocracy and so were forced to enjoy their fame rather more discreetly.

On Frinton's northern flank, by complete contrast are the Art Deco houses, conceived of by the architect, Oliver Hill, in early 1934. The ambitious Frinton Park Estate was born out of a rampant class snobbery. An article in a 1935 *Country Life* magazine waffles plummily on about the need to create 'a continental plage' as an antidote to "...the typical English seaside resort with its pier, bandstand and the smell of cigarettes on asphalt." There was to be nothing installed on the estate which might encourage "...the mass-descent of the weekend crowd." The article mentions the desirability that Frinton should be "well-kept and well-bred" and goes on to hope for "...the elimination of the vulgar plebs" – a thing which made your correspondent here burst into outraged laughter when he read it.

Hill's vision for Frinton Park – which included a luxury seafront hotel – was inspired by Monte Carlo, and other swish continental caravanserais favoured by the uber-rich of his period. The 200 acre estate was also intended as a showcase for British design, with much of the architectural elite of the day eagerly on board. As usual, though, proceedings were dogged by problems at every step. There were disputes with the local authority that, among other matters, quibbled over the proposed thickness of the concrete walls. Naturally, the architects also bickered with the project director. And then – just like today – everybody blamed the builders, until predictably, it all got woefully behind schedule and over budget. The company went bust in 1936 and Oliver Hill's dream capsized, leaving only a fragment of the 'Deauville in Essex' which he'd endeavoured to build. It's still a pretty impressive fragment, though. Essex's own Ozymandias, if you like.

The singer, Elvis Costello, once said that writing about music was like dancing about architecture. Frinton's Art Deco houses, though, probably are an example of architecture worth dancing about. Many of them, with their cubes, curves, rails, balconies and portholes look like they've been heisted wholesale from a luxury ocean liner. And they *do* still look futuristic. Estate agent spec of the time notes that some of their bathrooms had rubber floors and Vitrolite lining. Oh, and there was a bedsitting room for a maid. I know this because I studied a floor plan and one room says 'Maid' on it. That would definitely have swung the deal for me. I personally can't think of anything better after a hard day's work than a cruise home in the Laundalette – popping in at Connaught Avenue for a bottle of Bombay Gin? a bit of Jack Payne & the BBC Dance Orchestra on the wind-up gramophone and then – if no one's about – tap gently on the maid's door and ask her if she fancies a drink and a spot of dancing about architecture. Yes, I think I'd probably quite like that In fact I've asked the estate agent to notify me the minute that a place comes up on the market.

3. Jaywick

A bracing cycle ride from Clacton to Jaywick, I skirt the sea and whizz past the Never Say Die pub. All alleged stigmas aside, the little seaside village is a fiercely independent place, with a closer community than most. Jaywick's residents seem impervious to the general condescensions and handwringing, which for years they've had to endure from much of the surrounding world. You can buy a little house here for thirty-five thousand, or a three-bedroom one for just under forty thousand. Today people are out and about, buying newspapers and milk, leaning on their gates, chatting to neighbours and, well, generally behaving like a community does. Despite uncharitable things sometimes said about the place, much opinion in Jaywick itself, holds that it has no more social problems than many other places and feels that those which they do have, they can deal with themselves. I have occasionally worked in Jaywick over the years and have yet to be accosted by brigands here. Quite apart from this, the village has some of the cheapest and friendliest cafes in Essex, the best weather in England and their beach is the envy of much of the east coast. Jaywick Sands really are golden and enduringly popular with local holidaymakers. As an added bonus, this particular morning, there's the poetic sight on the horizon of a solitary Thames sailing barge breasting the sea's thrashing grey artex. What had begun as a tropically humid day further inland, begins to gather itself into a storm, and I stop by the Martello Tower to guess which way it might go.

Before its reinvention, Jaywick, like neighbouring Clacton, was once a simple hamlet. Its creator, Frank Stedman, bought the plot for £7,500 in 1928, opening it a year or so later as a holiday village, Jaywick Sands. Many of its chalets were built in classic 1930s style, echoing grander houses in the new garden cities, further west. Some of these chalets give a gabled nod to the architectural craze for all things Tudor at that time. Frank Stedman, a latterday edition of Peter Bruff , moved his entire family in to run what he called his "Jaywick Decision". Vestiges of his humour pervade the place. For instance, Jaywick's Brooklands area, when studied on a street map, reveals the shape of a Bentley radiator grille. Brooklands' street-names too, are themed on old cars: Sunbeam, Alvis and so on, while the roads which lead off Jaywick's main drag, Broadway, are named prettily after coastal flowers.

Soberingly, Jaywick, is billed as the third most-deprived area in England. Having worked in certain areas in the northeast, however, I find it to be a lot less edgy than its northern counterparts. It's true that some of Brooklands' side streets are overgrown and neglected, with a few houses boarded up or security grilled. Many more of the houses though, look homely and cared for. Perhaps, to some of its fussy neighbours, it may look scruffy. Clacton's attitude to Jaywick might be compared to that of *Keeping Up Appearances* Hyacinth Bucket's to her slipshod relatives, Daisy and Onslow. Exaggerated stories of burnt-out shanties, though, are usually circulated by Jaywick's crueler, erstwhile, visitors. I, myself, only pass one such place today, which, I think, was the same one that I saw when filming here a while ago.

The truth is that Jaywick needs serious investment. It has substantial drainage and flooding issues – and always has had. Frank Stedman and Clacton Council were arguing about the problems way back in 1928, before the first houses were even built. But matters were never resolved and, in the notorious 1953 floods, Jaywick was devastated, with 37 dead and 300 made homeless. It's important to remember, however, that Jaywick was only meant, initially, to be a holiday village. Residence became more permanent in the severe post-war housing shortage, when the village's predominantly East End settlers simply had nowhere else to go and the government of the day had nowhere else to send them. It's highly likely that a long entrenched sense of shared adversity is what has given Jaywick its famously tight-knit community spirit.

The estate agents like to call Jaywick 'West Clacton'. Well, they would, wouldn't they? Clacton and Jaywick, after all, are only separated by a golf course. Creasing the map? Estate agents? Surely not.

Recent hot news is that Jaywick has just been twinned. Not twinned internationally, like Colchester – with its stately bustled French counterpart, Avignon. No, Jaywick has been more modestly twinned, with Studd Hill, near Herne Bay in Kent – another of Frank Stedman's half-forgotten holiday spot creations. Studd Hill's house prices are higher, granted, but I bet Jaywick's got the better beach. Eight decades after it was built, you might wonder how Jaywick is doing. The answer is that Jaywick is doing fine. Jaywick is unique in fact, and has more friends and secret admirers than it probably knows.

4. Harwich

I could have stayed in for the day and perhaps I should have. At some point during the New Year I'd managed to download Version 1 of the National Cold into my system – that's the one that comes with the hacking cough and blocked sinus, with its optional pop-ups of headache and sore throat. It was a bright cold Saturday and I decided to go and mooch around in Harwich instead. When the god in charge of mucking about with perfectly good historical places visited Harwich, he must have missed a lot of it out. The old part of the town is remarkably untouched and still haunted by the ghosts of the thrumming old seaport that it used to be.

From the town pier, you can see the confluence of the rivers Orwell and Stour and imagine the numberless sailing ships over the centuries whose first or last sighting of England must have been old Harwich. It's a little-known fact that when the Beatles first went to Germany in August of 1960, for a 48-night stint at Hamburg's sleazy Indra Club, it was from Harwich that they left. There's a blurred snapshot in one of my old pop books, of John Lennon on the quay watching the band's battered and overloaded Austin van being hoisted onto the ferry.

For centuries, Harwich was a hugely significant port. Samuel Pepys, the naval administrator and diarist, was an MP here. When Dr. Johnson and Boswell left England for Holland, it was also from Harwich, which was then the gateway to Germany and the Low Countries. Daniel Defoe described the port as: "...a town of hurry and business, not much of gaiety and pleasure." but acknowledged that some of its residents were wealthy. The vestiges of that wealth are still to be seen in the streets of the old town, though the grandeur is discreet – as you might expect in a town which has also known hard times.

When I first knew Harwich in the mid-Seventies as a young pantywaist of a singer in a gigging band, it was known as a rufty-tufty, hard-living sort of place where you generally watched your step. My father was a Port Health Officer here for many years and was immensely fond of it. Later, however, after the sea cargoes were containerised and the trade moved away from the old port, it made him sad to revisit the place. When he met the old port workers he'd known, he said: "You find they just want to talk about the old days."

There's still a residual melancholy about the Old Town and yet one gets the feeling that Harwich is quietly beginning to flourish again. The American cruise ships arrive in summer – disgorging many of their passengers into Harwich for the day. True, many will be coached to Colchester or London for day-trips but others will stay and wander around the town marvelling at the antiquity of the buildings or gazing up at Harwich's imposing church, St. Nicholas. In addition to this, Christopher Jones, the Master of the Mayflower was from here. The Elizabethan house where he was born is in Kings Head Street. In nearby streets, even by contrast with ten or fifteen years ago, there are signs that Harwich is beginning to do okay. Some of the older houses, bought by hard-up teachers during the housing boom years, when Harwich was cheaper than many other places, look well kept and genteel. Despite dire times for the pub trade, there are still lots of pubs and, as one local told me, "It's not hard to find somewhere to eat here." The Pepys and the Pier restaurants both seem to be flourishing and, even on this bitterly cold day, if the streets are quiet it's only because the eateries are full. In high season, my guide said, on some days these streets are packed. And the people who really do take to Harwich are the cruise ships' mainly Filipino and Thai crews.

Standing on the town's Ha'penny Pier, it's easy to imagine Harwich as it once was: a place full of tall-masted ships, coal boats and men-of-war – many of which were built here for the Navy. Further in, in the alleyways and cut-throughs of the Old Town were the sailmakers, the chandlers, the taverns and the roperies. A few centuries ago, Harwich was the town that never closed. Here the press gang would have waited, to waylay some drunk sailor so that he could wake up with a headache en route to a sea battle with the Dutch navy. Here, Defoe arrived in spring of 1722, finding the townsmen: "Far from being famed for their good usage of strangers." Here too, the Huguenot refugees and Flemish weavers on their way to Colchester would have had their first experiences of England. Harwich was also the port where many thousands of Jewish refugees entered Britain after the rise of the Nazis. The old port had always loomed large. And then came the slump of the late 20th century when the economic game moved up the field. Harwich today though, surprises me and I can't think why I haven't been back here for so long. One thing that has gone from strength to strength during the past two decades is the town's famous independent cinema, The Electric Palace. This well-restored 1920s edifice continues to defy convention by showing all the films the rapacious and uncaring large cinema chains (which cater mainly for android viewing tastes) refuse to show. And, sure, there's talk in the town about the recent closure of Woolworths and what might disappear next. But despite the freezing weather there was a good turnout on the quay for the New Year fireworks. In a few months' time the cruise ships will be in again and the various festivals and tours will take place. Then the visitors will come – and I will be among them.

Chapter Twelve

Psycle-Geography – Clacton to the Naze

With August in, the summer's peaked, the evenings have cooled and the pollen count's come down. High time therefore, to leave the garret, get on the boneshaker and head for the coast. This time I decided to follow the coastal path from Clacton to Walton and the Naze Tower. I adore this bit of coastline and a bicycle has the appropriate height and speed with which to best see it. I arrive at the West Cliff Theatre while aimlessly pedalling around Clacton's sidestreets. It rears up at me suddenly, like a wodge of children's party cake plonked on the street corner. It's been at its Tower Road location since 1928 and has a fine showbiz history. The list of luminaries who've graced its stage over the past eight decades reads like a *Who's Who* of light entertainment. They've nearly all been here at some point in their careers. The theatre's original roots are Victorian and even Ernie Leno, son of the legendary Dan Leno once played here. The West Cliff has also hosted Stanley Holloway, Roy Hudd, Tommy Trinder, Billy Dainty, Don Maclean and countless others. As soon as I walk into its foyer, I sense that it is special – seaside special.

Ushered into its well-preserved 600-seat auditorium, two things strike me. Firstly, its appearance: still visible over the stage's proscenium archway are the gilt letters G&B – after Graham and Bentley, two of its founders. If you ever wanted to make a bio-pic about say, The Shadows, this would be the place to recreate the live scenes. It looks exactly as it must have done in the late 1950s when Hank and the boys were making their name. And it feels that way too – though there's no shabbiness or neglect about it. No surprise, therefore, to discover that early Brit rockers, Joe Brown and Marty Wilde still love to play here regularly. The second thing that I notice is the West Cliff's atmosphere. This is a well-loved place and even when it's empty, as it happens to be on this midweek morning, the silence seems loaded – as if a show had just this minute finished or was about to begin. It's almost like it's retained a little something from every trouper who ever trod its boards. I ask Mike Bareham, the

West Cliff's manager, if it's haunted: "There's a butterfly," he says, with no trace of irony. "Technicians and many other people see it fluttering around in the rafters and the lights." The peculiar thing is that it's seen all year round. Even in winter, when there shouldn't be any butterflies about.

The West Cliff, which is active for over 300 days a year, mostly does 'old days' entertainment. It's what puts rears on tiers, they've found. There are Sixties packages, there are Forties shows, there are family comedians from the Seventies and there are Summer Specials. These are the meat and potatoes on the West Cliff's menu. In an age of scant and fussy arts funding, the old place must fight its corner harder than most. Sure, they can apply for arts grants if they wish. But the funding gods do not beam sunnily upon such places. The West Cliff, you see, is a receiving theatre rather than a producing one. That is, they'll take a Summer Special or, say, The New Seekers but they won't produce a radical cutting-edge play This is partly because they daren't risk it. Clacton knows what it likes – and it's a wise theatre manager who knows his own audience.

"I did go up to Cambridge... once, " recalls Mike, referring to a time when he'd applied for arts funding. "But a woman who made rude sculptures of body parts got all the money." The kindly theatre manager tells me this fact with absolutely no chagrin, only a small shrug of bafflement. In the lofty minarets of arts funding, there's apparently a fine difference between clever and wrong. Entertaining those theatregoers of cherishable age with what they know and like is obviously 'wrong'. Whereas producing a bleak play about two Ukranian women arguing over a broken tractor would be 'clever' and could well net you the money to repair the theatre roof. Sure you might only have four punters and even then one of them might need to be Tasered back into his seat but you'd secure that all-important grant. He's a tricky customer, Johnny Arts-Funding, and as a man who once had to punch himself in the face in order to stay awake during an utterly wretched Strindberg play, I confess that I do have a few sympathies with the populist lobby.

The old place does have its supporters – not the least of these being Tendring District Council and the Friends of The West Cliff Theatre. Mike Bareham and his colleagues, though, still have to think on their feet to keep the place as painted as it's sainted. Coming up soon, for instance, is veteran comic, Jimmy Tarbuck.

Hot on his heels, the West Cliff hosts former Dr. Hook frontman,
Dennis Locorriere, whom I have known grown men to travel miles
for in order to be able to cry into their beers over his songs. Ticket
sales are going well. With that, still pondering upon the vast differ-
ences between clever and wrong, I straddle the boneshaker and
head for Walton-on-the-Naze.

It's incredible how well an old bicycle will do you. I mean, you
see all these chaps on ruinously expensive all-terrain bikes, with
their drinking bottles and on board computers. Then, because
they've bought the bikes, they have to wear the gear as well – the
ergonomic helmet, the lycra suit and shades. What they actually
look like, from a distance, though, are large chubby ants in shiny
blue Babygros. We're in Essex, remember? A girl's second-hand
shopper bike would probably do you for most of the county and if
you do come across a bit of a hill, well, you can always get off and
push.

With a fair tailwind behind me, I'm on a creaky old 5-speed
Raleigh, ripping along the designated coastal route through
Clacton, heading for the mid-Hannoverian charms of the Naze
Tower. The path is about five and half miles long, mostly flat and a
pleasure to do. Once I'm out of central Clacton, to my surprise, I
hardly meet anyone, apart from a few gaffers performing the late
morning dog walk. Clacton melds gradually into Holland-on-Sea
and the path becomes a track as I skirt the Frinton Golf Club, eventually finding myself in Frinton itself. There's a very pleasing soundtrack while I'm doing all this. It's a particular echo carried on the
wind of English holiday beaches: children, dogs, seagulls and the
sea. It's a highly evocative sort of sound, which they ought to sell in
record shops under the title *East Coast Ambient* for old jades who need
to get their souls back. It works for me, anyway.

Of all the seaside towns on the Tendring Peninsula, Walton-on-
the-Naze is the one I know least well. Peter Bruff had business here
too. He pulled out of the project, though, before realising his dream
of building a tramway between here and neighbouring Frinton. At
2,600 feet, Walton's pier is the third longest in the country. The original one, built in 1830, was also one of the earliest such structures.
The town's popularity reached its zenith in Victorian times, and its
decline as a holiday resort was accelerated by the Second World
War, when the pier was shortened and the town took a series of

pastings from enemy aircraft. It made brave attempts to recover afterwards but never regained its earlier popularity. If some of the holidaymakers from farther afield didn't return, however, Walton is held in very high esteem locally. In a coastal triumvirate including Clacton and Frinton, it is Walton which I hear spoken of most affectionately by people in this area. They think of it as friendly, still relatively unchanged and fun. As I cycle down into the little seaside town, it does have that sort of timeless atmosphere. Near to lunchtime on a weekday morning, the High Street is buzzing, the shops are busy and the place feels like it's on holiday.

I'm headed for the Naze Tower though, so I'm not hanging around today. About a mile up the road on the windy cliffs of the ever-crumbling Naze, it looms up ahead of me. The Naze Tower was built between 1740 and 1741. At the time, George II was on the throne, Robert Walpole was PM and we'd just begun a war with a very silly name indeed – The War of Jenkin's Ear. The tower, that is octagonal and 86-feet high, was built by Trinity House as a navigational aid for shipping. It has had a number of owners and changes of use since. Interestingly enough, the Naze Tower was once an 18th century tearoom. This was in days when tea was an expensive commodity, which had to be smuggled into the country from Holland. A tearoom and art gallery is what the tower has reverted to now and is probably how the place will end its days, too.

When I arrive, Michelle Nye-Brown and her assistant are serving teas and light refreshments to a constant stream of customers. Michelle's family bought the Naze Tower in 1996, opening it to visitors a few years later, after substantial restoration work. The place wasn't too expensive either because, apparently, if certain vital sea defences aren't undertaken soon, within the next two decades the tower will go the way of the wartime pillbox, and end up on its side down on the beach below. The Naze is a Site of Special Scientific Interest and the Naze Protection Society (NPS) currently needs to raise £800,000 to prevent the Naze and its tower from being lost to the ravenous North Sea. They've raised a quarter of that sum so far.

Furnished by Michelle with a pair of binoculars, I climb the 111-step spiral staircase, over seven levels to the top of the tower and am suitably awestruck by the view. From here, laid out before me are views of Walton Backwaters, Felixtowe, Harwich and further out, if mistier, Orford Ness. On a really clear day, it's said, you can see the south Kent coast. It's an unforgettable experience, though not one which I'd recommend to anyone with vertigo. I gaze down at the greensward miles below and imagine tricorn-hatted Georgians on breezy summer days watching a sea dotted with tall masted ships leaving old Harwich. It's often said that this country is a small one. Some days it can seem absolutely vast.

Chapter Thirteen

Martyrs On The Railings

*When you talk to an artist
That's a penny to a pound
He's turned his mental grill orf
Afore his toast was browned*

In the first few years that I lived in Wivenhoe, there was an artist who lived up the road. He sometimes wore his long hair under a sort of Jacobin-style woollen hat. I'd see him occasionally in the Rose and Crown smoking a Sherlock Holmes pipe. He was in his late twenties – a few years older than me. He had a striking sort of face – one that was rather handsome. Another striking thing about him was his long black leather coat and the women's tights he wore. His air was one of distinguished distraction and to look at him you'd think he might have had rather a posh voice when he spoke. In fact, when I did get to know him, his accent actually had a cockney twang to it. One summer, I saw him sitting on the quay, shirtless and absolutely covered in insect bites. He'd been painting in the woods all day, he said. I saw one of his paintings, once. It depicted a bloody medieval battle with a crazy-eyed warrior triumphantly holding up a sword in the foreground. I was really impressed that anyone nowadays would paint such an epic thing. It wasn't what I'd expected at all. One story I heard about this artist concerned the large communal house where he lived in the High Street and under whose sign, Gothic House, he'd painted the legend: *"Home of the Brave."*

He'd had some sort of an argument about noise with the couple who lived downstairs from his quarters. One night, near the stroke of midnight, while the couple lay in their bed, the door crashed open. There the artist stood, framed in the doorway – naked except for a viking helmet and his boots. He was holding a battle-axe above his head and screaming: "Yaaaarrrrrgh!" It was probably his idea of a joke and the incident didn't go any further but the couple was suitably terrified and I heard that they'd moved out soon afterwards. This story quietly did the rounds of the few people who knew him and was the source of much merriment among us all. It was how, from everything I'd learned so far, I had *hoped* an artist might behave. He came round to my house once, dressed in his unconventional style. My then six year-old stepdaughter asked her mother later, "Mummy, why is that man wearing tights?" So far, so lower Wivenhoe.

Wivenhoe has a reputation for being an arty place. In summer you may sometimes catch Tessa Spenser-Pryse RA, with her easel set up somewhere in sunny Alma Street, catching the light that filters through the leaves of the overhanging lime trees. You may also, occasionally, see Charles Debenham in the churchyard mapping out some new painting. In fact, you will often see people sketching or drawing, around the streets or the river. Many of them don't live in Wivenhoe.

Also, in the summer, there's an event called *Art On The Railings* held in the churchyard. Here are watercolours – challenged or otherwise – plus pastel paintings, oil paintings and others. The paintings are all mounted on the church railings and sold. Also arrayed round the churchyard are many stalls. There are second-hand bookstalls, cake stalls, stalls selling tomato plants grown from seed, stalls selling bric-a-brac and much other stuff that has been exhumed from lofts and garages. In among it all, an elderly trio led by a keyboard player sets up and plays old jazz standards. They do it rather well. It's pleasant to listen to as it floats up the High Street on the summer air. It is a quintessentially provincial English experience and corny as it may sound in my description, it's a perfectly delightful sort of way to spend a Saturday morning. I hardly ever miss it. I usually come away with four tomato plants, three paperbacks and a wine demijohn.

I never buy any art though. Why? Well, firstly, because the walls of my tiny house are as full of art as they possibly can be. In common with many long-term Wivenhoe residents, I have gradually amassed a collection of various paintings and drawings, either done by friends, or bought for me as presents. Secondly, some of the art on display in the churchyard, with the best will in the world, is fit only for the walls of a seaside B&B. A few years ago I wouldn't have recognised this fact. I knew nothing about art, apart from the fact that I knew what I *didn't* like. Now, thanks to living in Wivenhoe and having been dragged, nagged or cajoled into going to so many exhibitions, I begin at least to have some idea of whether it's been well done or not. I remain at heart, however, the kind of guy who mostly likes pictures of stags in glens, or kittens in a boot. So what do I know?

It was way back in the early 1970s when I first encountered some of the Wivenhoe artists. I met Tony Young, Pam Dan and her husband John, Michael Heard, Roy Cross and his wife Gail. They were as disparate a group of people as a young man could meet. Tony Young, who had flirted with anarchism when he was younger, was a friendly and affable sort of bloke. When I first clapped eyes on him, to me, he looked vaguely nautical. Tall and rather handsome with a neat dark beard, he might easily have been mistaken for the skipper of a charter yacht. He'd come up from St Ives, in Cornwall. After art college though, he'd worked in advertising in London and at some point had dropped out of the business, eventually becoming something of a lotus-eater here in the 1960s. Now, or when I knew him at least, he did some portraiture and sometimes painted thin and rather boyish young female models. He also made some pin money by framing pictures. He was a keen CND and Labour Party activist and, of course, he was fond of a drink or three. Towards the end of his life – he was only round about sixty years old – he'd mellowed considerably and was held in huge affection by the regulars in the Greyhound, where bar staff knew him as Uncle George. Like Billy the Fish, Tony left rather a hole in Wivenhoe pub life when he shuffled off the coil.

Gail Cross had been a Chelsea Girl and was scarily beautiful when she was younger. Even up until a few years before her death in March of 1998, she still had a certain charisma and charm about her. Her husband Roy was regarded as a good painter. As a young art teacher in his native Liverpool he'd taught John Lennon and Stuart Sutcliffe at Liverpool School of Art. He too was a handsome fellow, who often favoured wearing dark clothes. With his sweptback hair he was mildly redolent perhaps of a young Johnny Cash. When the pair first came to the town they made a striking couple and I have heard them spoken of, only partly in jest, as a sort of Burton-Taylor of Wivenhoe.

Michael Heard was the first artist who befriended me in this town. A wiry former army officer, he had a wild side to him and a well-attested reputation for volatility. Despite this, he was only ever

kindly to me – dispensing the odd bit of wisdom if I was ever having a struggle with my music and my own artistic path. And he was
usually good for a yarn, if I ever wandered into the Station Hotel
and found him perched upon his customary stool at the corner of
the bar. Michael was also interesting to me because, when he was-
n't being irascible, he possessed something of a mystical side to him.
His main artistic pieces – those which most people were familiar
with at any rate – were finely done, belt-and-braces paintings of the
quayside and boats. In the last decade of his life, however, he began
to turn out very different, almost psychedelic pieces. Some people
found the paintings strange and bemusing. One or two of us,
though, took them seriously or, at least, considered them to be interesting. Michael seemed to be onto something new. He was certainly very enthusiastic about them and I think the change of style
rather liberated him, lifting him out of his doldrums for a while. He
died whilst I was working away from the town and it was sad for me
to come back, on the day after his funeral, and find the whole affair
more or less wrapped up. After all, it was his son Sam whom I'd first
ever come to Wivenhoe with, in 1973. It felt like a salient chess piece
had been removed from the board whilst I'd momentarily glanced
away.

John Dan was a potter – a very good one too. Something I discovered, long after his death, was a strange mock-classical fresco
which he'd painted in the basement of the Old Rectory, where
William Dean, the village doctor had lived. It depicted some sort of
a classic Romano-Grecian revel complete with naked women and
wine jugs. I never did find out why it was there but it was very
Wivenhoe. It betokened an earlier bohemian time in the town.
John's widow, Pam, was and still *is* a painter, who in her time has
taught many other people to draw and paint. Of these six people,
Pam is the only one who now survives and is still working and regularly exhibiting as an artist.

But exactly *how* arty is Wivenhoe now? Whisper this heresy, but
are not Rowhedge or Manningtree equally arty? Of course they are.
It's just that Wivenhoe shouts about it a little louder. Wivenhoe is
Freddie Mercury to Rowhedge's Chris Rea or Manningtree's Mark
Knopfler. This is supposing for one demented moment that small
Essex riverside towns were 1980s rock stars which, of course, they
aren't. Though, hold that image for a minute.

Wivenhoe's abiding legend is its long-defunct Arts Club, opened by Edward Heath in 1970. I drew a fusillade of disapproval the last time I wrote anything about the Arts Club. An editor of a local magazine asked me to write something provocative in order to boost the mag's flagging readership. "What might we do?" he asked. "Slaughter a sacred cow?" I replied. I did a flip hatchet job on the Arts Club. In the subsequent article I asked that if they were all so brilliant, where had the great work of the 1960s got to? Had the artists really done any work? Had they not just engaged in a bloody great jolly up instead? Finally, I called them "The Boozebury Group" and wrote them off with a stroke of a smoking pen.

Dumber and dumber. The article drew me nearly two full pages of vitriol by return-of-pissed. (Sorry, that should have read 'return-of-post'.) The mag's entire run sold out almost immediately. I didn't defend myself of course. My work was done here. It was *Day of The Jackal* all over again. In fact for the duration of this exercise, I *was* Dave the Jackal. I'd thrown myself on a grenade for the purposes of circulation. It wasn't entirely fair of me to do so and it took about a decade for certain people to even bring themselves to speak to me again.

The real truth of the matter is that the Wivenhoe Arts Club, in its own time, loomed huge in the little town. As I was to discover later, it wasn't important for what it produced as such – although it *had* produced work. Much of this was sold at the time and now resides in various private collections. The thing about the Arts Club – situated in an old coach house adjoining its founder George Gale's house – was its gregariousness and its inclusiveness. It bothered to invite the neighbours in to all of its parties. It became very much a community thing. Here, people like Farmer John Bowes and Tony Allcock, the electrical shop-owner, met artists for the first time. The Arts Club held exhibitions, parties and extraordinary events. They even had an orchestra perform a concert there once. It is only when you talk to people like John and Tony that you begin to realise the impact that the Arts Club had on what was then pretty much a small, post-war rural community. All manner of people met all manner of other, very different people. Sometimes, it changed their lives. George Gale, then a top-notch London journalist and editor, brought his friends from London to the Arts Club. The Arts Club too, had its own late licence and also, according to legend, fostered a number of sub-Bacchanalian revels. Hadn't Michael Parkinson popped in occasionally? Were there not other luminaries in and out of the place over the years? Was it not dappled occasionally with genuine glamour? Yes – all of this and more. Suffice it to say that the club's existence added something of an exotic texture to the wider town's social fabric and helped make Wivenhoe the distinctively tolerant and differently wired place that it now is. When your farmers, brickies and fishermen have become drunk alongside the likes of Francis Bacon, George Gale or Dickie Chopping, only good can come out of it – for both sides. But art and the arts in general had existed *outside* of the Arts Club long before the club's arrival.

Chapter Fourteen

John, Dicky and Angie

"The Bond artist has died" proclaimed the headlines, one summer morning in 2008. Richard Chopping – 'Dicky' to everyone in lower Wivenhoe who knew him – had been frail for some years. If you met him on the street or in a shop, he might firstly regale you with a litany of his medical travails. He'd earned the right, though. At well past ninety, he'd led a life and a half. Steer him onto almost any subject other than the nuisance of his declining health and he would be by turns outrageous, erudite and incredibly nice. His legend was that he'd illustrated the original and now-iconic covers of nine James Bond books, a thing which, although it made him internationally famous, had ended in an acrimonious row over royalties with their author, Ian Fleming. But quite apart from this, Dicky was – to paraphrase the great Quentin Crisp – one of the East Anglia's stateliest homos.

Towards the end of the last war, he and his friend and partner, Denis Wirth-Miller moved into a large quayside house in Wivenhoe, then needing much work done on it. They started as they meant to go on: they painted, they taught and they partied like there was no tomorrow. The artist Francis Bacon would often pop up for the weekend to stay and work in a cottage which they also owned in nearby Queens Road. The actor, Wilfred Bramble, of *Steptoe & Son* fame, would arrive. All manner of carry-on and general whoopsie-daisy occurred. Stories were rife, for instance, about Bramble in the 1960s, being chased naked round Anchor Hill during the drunken small hours. Many of the tales concerning their revels are simply unprintable. More still, however, chronicle the two artists' kindness, lack of snobbery and general entertainment value. They owned several properties in the village, which, in the days when houses were still places to live rather than investment portfolios, they rented out at reasonable rates to townspeople. The ordinary working folk of the little riverside town – even in those pre-permissive, post-war decades – not only accepted them but, for the most part, held the pair in affectionate esteem. Part of this might have stemmed from the fact that Dicky Chopping was definitively from "round here". Dicky had been born in Colchester just before the Great War and his family had owned Chopping Mill in the mid-19th century. The Fingringhoe mill – now a private dwelling – was a Gormenghast of a place, which loomed out of the marshes in the low mist across the River Colne opposite their Regency house as a reminder of this heritage.

Hardly anything Dicky ever said of anyone was commonplace. "She smells of sex," he'd pronounced bluntly of one young femme fatale then resident in the village. Or: "I have to tell you – you look like a bloody Giacometti when you dress all in black," he'd greeted me with one summer morning, whilst I was cutting a hedge in the High Street. Late one night, he said, he had interrupted a couple "going at it like hammer and tongs" outside his house and remonstrated with them for making too much noise: "Wassamatter, Grandad – wanna join in?" the man had sneered. "Thirty years ago," riposted Dicky in cracked tones, "I might have done. Only, not with her – with you."

One Sunday night in the bloodshot-eyed '70s – well after last bells – the two Wivenhoe artists had rolled off the last London train into the Station Hotel. With them was Francis Bacon, a Staffordshire bull terrier of a man, sporting a tightly cinched trench coat and a black eye. They were all hammered. They ordered drinks for the whole house and were duly served. Dicky's partner Denis patted his pockets and licked his lips. "I don't suppose..." he began. Incredibly, the landlord immediately advanced him the money for the continuation of what looked like an epic debauch. "How the hell did they wangle that one?" your young correspondent here asked. They were gentlemen, a local replied and the landlord knew that their credit was good. They were indeed gentlemen. When the monstrously famous Francis Bacon died a few years later, as the media vultures and panhandlers circled the place for stories, they were met by Dicky and Denis with arms stacked and lips sealed. Nobody was spilling the beans.

They'd met absolutely everyone of course. Of the Great Beast, Aleister Crowley, for instance, Dicky had said: "Didn't we once spend an evening with him in the south of France, Denis? Silly little man." They'd been in all the right places – and quite a few of the wrong ones too – at all of the right times. And yet, invited into their house and shown its secret, walled garden, nestled at the back of Anchor Hill, you might marvel at the plants, their pots and the ordered sculpture of it all. They had green fingers and kept an equally secret garden around the corner in Brook Street, with beautifully tended espaliered pears. They were charming men. They knew so much about these things. At the heart of it, after all, was the solid, if occasionally seismic, bedrock of a long and successful domestic partnership. With the passing of Dicky Chopping, went not only a part of the 20th century but also a splash of vibrant colour on the largely monochrome England of his times – an England which George Orwell described as a place where, in theory, everything was forbidden but in reality anything might happen. That Essex should have spawned such a fellow as "the Bond artist" is to its eternal credit. Though Dicky wasn't by any means the first luminary that Wivenhoe spawned.

On the wall of an elegant house in Rose Lane, opposite the side entrance of the Rose and Crown pub is a blue plaque. It commemorates the actor-manager Sir John Martin Harvey (1863-1944). The most common picture you'll find of Sir John is one taken of him in a dramatic pose as Sydney Carton in *The Only Way* – a highly successful stage adaptation of *A Tale of Two Cities*. He's wearing dandyish apparel and a stunningly rakish cocked hat. His are the watery, haunted eyes of a doomed Sixties pop star. His clothes in the picture – stage clothes actually – might just as well have been my own in the mid 1980s when I still played in rock bands. Showbiz, the arts, rock music and theatres are the only homes for such driven creatures.

John was born in Wivenhoe, the son of John Harvey, a well-known ship-builder and yacht designer. Naturally, John Harvey the elder wanted young John to follow in his footsteps (just as the old Terry Newell wanted the young Martin to follow in *his* footsteps and join the British Army). But it was just never going to happen. A look at this young man's eyes even when he was nine years old would probably have told you all that you'd needed to know about his destiny. He was headed for nowhere but the limelight. And when they knighted John Martin Harvey in 1921, aged 58, he was feted as one of the last great romantic theatre actors of his age. Not bad for a boy born in Bath Street, Wivenhoe.

We have writers too, although they generally tend to be a little less visible. In lower Wivenhoe, for years, has lived an extraordinary woman called Leila Berg. She's actually a famous and revered children's author, an indefatigable campaigner for children's rights and a former Morning Star journalist. If you ever catch sight of this tiny wren of a woman, you would never guess that in her younger feistier days, she was a left-wing firebrand who had lost not one, but two lovers to the Spanish Civil War before she even married. I have a signed book of hers somewhere in the house. In fact, having read one of my own books, she once told me off in the street for my sloppy prose – a thing that I'm enduringly proud of.

Another famous children's author was Mary Norton, creator of *The Borrowers* and *Bedknobs and Broomsticks*. She lived for a while at West Street, in a weatherboarded house opposite Quay Street. So far as I can gather, she lived here in the 1960s and she lived here so quietly that I've been unable to track down much about her at all. She moved to Ireland in 1972 and lived *there* pretty quietly too, before dying in 1992. That's the thing about writers. We're mostly girly swots, working indoors and often going quietly bonkers trying to write the rent. I'm sure that most people think that we're away all week being served canapés at literary launches in London – or wandering mountain fastnesses staring into limpid dewponds and crying at tiny flowers. Most of us though, only manage about three days of the year engaged in those types of activities. The rest of the time it's actually long days of hard graft at the newly digitised literary coalface.

In Wivenhoe, in fact, are playwrights, historians, journalists, editors and literary allsorts. I know that many of us would love to spend more time off our faces on absinthe and laudanum, chasing each other round the streets naked, having rows about form and trying to maim each other with knives and unreliable firearms. It was what they all did in the old days, wasn't it? But you see, we just don't get the time nowadays. Occasionally we'll meet, sure – usually in the Post Office, or at Art on the Railings. We never talk about work. What would we say to each other? "Wow! I did some amazing cross-referencing today!"

Actually, I think Wivenhoe would be better off having something called *Martyrs On The Railings*.

Once a year, everyone who moans about the arts being "so dumbed-down nowadays" could be tied to the church railings in their hessian gowns on a rain-lashed summer Saturday. Then, while they wailed and gnashed their teeth, stalls could be set up around them selling fairy cakes and tomato plants, while a cheery jazz ensemble vamped away in the corner. It would work for me anyway. Yes, Wivenhoe has all its artists, writers, musicians, sculptors, directors, objectors, fixers and shiksas. And it has me – Mart on the Railings.

Wivenhoe also has Angie Diggens – the Last of the Showgirls. She too, has her story. The Last of the Showgirls sits on a sofa in her nan's bunglalow and tells me that the West End is not where she wants to end up. Over the past few years – since she made the national finals of *Stars In Their Eyes*, aged only seventeen – she has made Essex her stronghold. Angie Diggens, at all of twenty years old is the polar opposite of Amy Winehouse. No rehab, no hair-apocalypses and no visits to the Self-harmers' Market for her. She works, she works and then she works. It's turned into a family industry. Dad, Neil, is soundman, her mum, Julia, does PR and Nan helps with the costumes. Her family are all local – Wivenhoe, Elmstead Market and round about. They are ordinary, grounded people with no previous showbiz connections as such. Angie has sung, played, danced, acted, taught and directed shows since she was a young girl. She will *never* do nine-to-five, she says – and you believe her. While other young women of her age with any showbiz leanings join hopeless indie bands, or queue to be ritually humiliated in regional heats for TV unreality shows, the Last of the Showgirls has already seized control of her destiny and is running with it like a Teuton to a poolside sunlounger.

She puts on her own self-written, self-financed musicals at Clacton's West Cliff Theatre. She has also performed at Colchester's Mercury Theatre. She auditions the young cast herself, writes the scripts and is usually to be found frantically rehearsing and choreographing the casts of her productions. This is her own money, which she earned herself and she fully expects to recoup production costs. When she plays Clacton it's usually to full houses. If you know this trade, you'll also know that this is a rather neat trick, if you can pull it off.

Angie Diggens is also big on something called the 'Organ Circuit'. She plays one of those all-singing, all-dancing electronic organs that won't quite fit in a hatchback – even with the seats down. It is *The Organist Entertains* made incarnate, as her hands flutter over the twin keyboards and her feet dance daintily over the bass pedals. She can play you the theme from *633 Squadron* and a number of hits that your blue-haired mother might know. It is strangely moving when I ask her to play me the *Dambusters March* and she does it. She can sing – really sing. I ask her, did her appearance in the national finals of *Star In Their Eyes* boost her career? It was good for local publicity she says. Ooh, and she was asked to do a showjumper's wedding in Ireland. She adds that she really didn't want to become a Sarah Brightman tribute act and had turned down offers to do so.

In an era when everyone from farmers' daughters to provincial call centre workers can't wait to karaoke their vulgar way into show-biz, show off their tattooed bottoms on TV and then marry a foot-baller, Angie has taken that rutted and pitted old back road called Variety. She is the compleat family entertainer. If a nuclear bomb were ever to hit the Sunshine Variety Club, taking out all of Britain's venerable troupers – your Brucies and your Cillas – Angie could single-handedly rebuild that world for you. I ask the Last of the Showgirls what her ultimate ambition is and where she would like to end up? Clear-eyed, she tells me that she'd like to do cruises, maybe open her own theatrical school and to continue touring. I glance at her gig list, which is formidably long. And then I remember that she'd rehearsed the previous night until 10 pm. I consider how tired she must be. She doesn't look it. How many 20 year-olds are this focused, this sorted out? Would that be your querulous, drunken son, Sir? Or perhaps your truculent, self-pitying daughter, Madam?

Study the gallery on Angie's website and it is awash in pictures of her with stone grey mayors, civic dignitaries, theatre bosses and heads of charities. They all look pleased to be there – rather like tribal chiefs might be, if photographed standing next to Princess Anne. In full slap, she is possessed of a genuine glamour. Our silver citizens adore her. In Southend, in Clacton, at Great Bromley and in all the parish halls where Amy Winehouse and Pete Doherty never go, she is simply 'their Angie'. For them, she is an eiderdown of talent upon the cold lumpy futon of modern entertainment. The Last of the Showgirls says that money isn't her main motivation. She adds that, ideally, she'd like to tour with her own company. It's honest actor-manager stuff – a bit like Sir John Martin Harvey.

Her mother, Julia, insists that I see a video of Angie's cast doing: *If My Friends Could See Me Now*. My first thought was that the entire Arts Council Executive should be sat down and made to watch it and then asked why it was any less eligible for funding than say, Native American percussion workshops for schools, or a Chekhov play, come to that? They would not, of course, even consider her and Angie wouldn't dream of approaching them. The Last of the Showgirls and the metropolitan arts elite are unlikely ever to interface.

Angie Diggens might well be Sir John Martin Harvey's legitimate successor. I deliberately draw no distinction between any of the artistes whom I've mentioned in these chapters about Wivenhoe's arts world. To me it's all just a happy borsch of arts and entertainments. There should be no delineations made in the great struggle to put food on our tables – not for scribblers, strummers, daubers or hoofers. Because, like Angie, in our own ways we're all just showgirls, really. And some of us get to pay the rent – if we're very, very lucky. The town of Wivenhoe is a good place for us to live. Because unlike certain other towns, the wider population is inured to our quirks, tolerant of our faults and, at times, quietly appreciative and supportive of our work. And it is the great Sir John Martin Harvey, charming old Dicky Chopping and the Wivenhoe Arts Club whom we partly have to thank for this.

Chapter Fifteen

As God As It Gets – The Church

I have never been a church-going sort of person. Unusually, too, no one on either my mother's or my father's side of the family ever went to church – at least not in my lifetime. After my father died, I found among his possessions a small book: *Common Prayer and Hymns Ancient & Modern*. It was given to him by his mother, on his ninth birthday. She had written in it: *To Terry from Mother. Mar. 22nd 1936 "Be thou faithful unto death and I will give thee the crown of life."*

Eight years afterwards, in November of 1944, with her son now a young recruit in the Buffs, my fifty-two year old grandmother was killed by a German V2 bomb while shopping in Woolworths in New Cross, London. If my father ever had a faith – which I believe he once did – this may have been the point at which he lost it.

While identifying her body, in Deptford Town hall – which he had to do from a scrap of her coat and her wedding ring – he stood with an older man, who had lost his wife in the bombing. A church-man of some sort did the rounds of the bereaved and said: "The Lord giveth and the Lord taketh away." The older man was very angry at such glibness, my father said, and had to be restrained by others present. With his elder brother away in Africa and his own father re-enlisted in the army and posted to the North-West Frontier in India, my seventeen-year-old dad was now alone in the world. He had one other task. He collected his dog – which had been in his mother's charge and which now had no one to care for it – and had it put down, before returning to his barracks near Aldershot. Within a few weeks he himself was posted to the North-West Frontier. The most poignant thing about it all, he said, was that his mother had been the family lynchpin. "When we all eventually got home after the war, the family never really reconvened again."

My father fought the army *not* to go on church parade and was set 'jankers'– cleaning toilets – for his youthful defiance, until he eventually appealed to a high-ranking superior officer and was left to his own godlessness. He spoke rather contemptuously of "Four-wheeler Christians", those who only went to church in a pram, a wedding car or a hearse and hardly attended at any other time. And yet, he sometimes used biblical quotes, which indicated that at some time, probably under the auspices of his mother, he had absorbed Christian ideals. He also taught me to respect the faith of others – particularly the Sikhs and the Moslems – whom he had garnered some knowledge of during his army career.

On my mother's side, the matter of God never came up. No one in the Wright family ever seemed to go to church. My grandfather, a cheery bus driver, was reportedly to be seen working in his shirt sleeves on the car on Sunday mornings during the 1930s, whilst neighbours in his street went tutting past on their way to church. My two brothers and I were never christened, my parents weren't married in a church and my father's funeral was the most austere that I've ever attended. And yet, in every other way, we were a strangely moral sort of family. Lying, stealing, or any kind of covetousness was deeply frowned upon. Consideration, courtesy and kindness to both neighbours and strangers were always practised. Working hard was to be admired. Retribution for bad behaviour was tough and forgiveness was eventual. During my own childhood, at least, swearing and blasphemy rarely occurred in the household. Greed and worship of profit or power were scorned. I was brought up, therefore, roughly upon Christian lines. It was just that – apart from hymns and prayers in school assembly – I was generally unfamiliar with *actual* Christian teaching or worship of any sort.

Whilst being almost completely ignorant about it, I have always liked the idea of a Church of England existing. It didn't seem as cruel or strict as certain other Christian faiths. I have had no cause to hate it or to reject the Church, as certain of my friends and acquaintances who were brought up under its aegis seem to do. The Anglican faith didn't seem rabid or angry. Its dominant image always seemed to me to be a kindly, if somewhat ineffectual, one. I associated it with blameless things such as church fetes, whist drives, jumble sales and blankets donated for disaster areas. Anglican hymns, with their rollicking melodies and descending bass lines are some of the best tunes I've ever heard and were my first musical influences. You can hear traces of these hymns in the music of The Beatles, The Who and, especially, The Beach Boys, as well as in my own music. I've sometimes stopped outside churches to hear the hymns, to listen to how the bass, treble and middle lines of the

organ seem to lace up so well within their main theme. Church of
England vicars – more so than the churchmen of other denomina-
tions – also seem to have more of a freedom to be quietly eccentric
or to do whatever is necessary to blend in with their flock.

Wivenhoe's St. Mary's Church is a good example of a traditional, provincial C of E church. Highly active in the local community,
it has a definite presence of its own and even those, like myself, who
don't attend it for worship, generally think well of it. At the time of
this writing, its rector, the Reverend David Thomas, after about sixteen years or so in Wivenhoe, is moving on. As I observed in earlier
accounts, David is a good man to have on your side at a wedding or
a funeral. Even atheists and those who may have fallen by the way-
side at some point in their lives, are seen out of the world with
respect and attention to the finer details of the lives which they
lived.

We live in spiritually bankrupt times. As a result of this, death
is now as great a modern taboo to us as sex was to the Victorians.
Many people nowadays pluck ingredients for their spiritual well-
being from a hotpotch of New Age mysticism, magic, and exotic
foreign faiths. It's almost as if they're taking pieces from so many
broken jigsaws and hoping to assemble a composite picture, which
might help them to make sense of the mystery of their own mortal-
ity. The Church, seemingly helpless in the face of this born-again
primitivism, can only watch its fluctuating attendance figures and
try to be on hand for those members of their scattered flock who
might stray back to the fold as a result of bereavement, ill health or
old age. God as a Great Bearded Dad, has somehow been usurped
by the ultimately less awesome Sea of Faith.

And yet, the Church goes on. People are still hatched, matched
and despatched under its rafters. The hymns are hardly less stirring
for not being belted out by a full house. And the Reverend David
Thomas, while some of his superiors stumble from one media PR
disaster to another is as popular a churchman as you may find in the
whole kingdom. When I talked to him, he disagreed that congrega-
tions were dwindling. In his opinion, he said, they'd reached 'a
plateau'. People arrived at their middle years and began to drift
back to the Church for one reason or another.

I don't know whether David is a typical clergyman, or even
whether there *is* such a thing as a typical clergyman, but he is certainly a man of his time. Like me, he's a baby-boomer, having been

born exactly halfway through the 20th century. He grew up, he says, with a soundtrack of the Beatles, the Rolling Stones, the Searchers et al and he loved the music. Although, as he recalls, he never went to many of the concerts. Amusingly – to me anyway – he admits to being: " More of a Stones man than a Beatles fan". This, too, is typical of a music fan of his age, that anyone younger wouldn't even know that there was once a schism between the two musical camps gives the fact away.

David Thomas grew up in north London and is a keen Arsenal fan: "I ran the flag up the pole at the church when they won the double in '98." he laughs. David also plays a pretty good game of pool and can be enticed out by his parishioners for a few frames in his free time. In fact, he was playing pool in a pub, the very first time I ever met him. At some time during the 1990s, a visiting group of burly working men arrived in the poolroom of my local pub, the Greyhound. I didn't recognise any of them and asked another local who they were. They were old mates of our new vicar, I was told. A mini-bus full of his former parishioners from Canvey Island had come up to visit him for a pint and to play pool with him. I thought this augured well for his future in Wivenhoe.

Nowadays, though, when so many people are without any sort of a faith at all, it's surprising how many will still leave the world – or have their dearly departed leave the world – under the steady gaze of the Church. This must present occasional difficulties for a rector, who may hardly have known the deceased as a worshipper. If, therefore, the funeral service of a non-attender ever seems to be somewhat off-the-peg, it's not entirely fair to blame the clergyman for it. Though I have never seen David Thomas conduct a funeral – even for some of the godless bohemians whom I have known and loved – that wasn't personalised in some way. For a population comprising roughly ten thousand souls, David conducts about forty funerals a year. He knows far more about his wider flock – even those that never come into the pen to be counted – than one might at first assume.

I say this because, occasionally, I too get asked to write a few words or a poem for someone who's passed on. This is a scary responsibility and when I first ever did it, with an unfamiliar quaver in my speaking voice, I began to get some sense of the amount of equilibrium a working clergyman must possess.

A few years ago, there were three funerals of people whom I knew – all in the space of a few weeks. I said to David at the time: "I'm getting to do nearly as many gigs here as you, lately." I later shortened this to a more showbiz-style: "Many in tonight?" It was a joke, of course. Possibly one in poor taste but it offset my general nervousness. I used to be more scared of getting up in church in front of my fellow mourners than almost any other event I'd ever done. I noticed that David had always done his homework too. I had to admire this. For David Thomas is a man charged with stewarding his flock between what the Irish call 'the two immensities' – birth and death. Whereas *I* only do gigs. No one will really mind if I cock it up. If David Thomas were to fluff one of his 'gigs', it *would* matter – big-time.

St. Mary's is what the author Anthony Everitt calls 'a community church'. At the artist Richard Chopping's funeral, David said: "Everybody is welcome in this church – *of all faiths and of none.*" Ronald Blythe, the author, once explained to me about the multiple early uses of Blythburgh Church in Suffolk. "In medieval times, the floor would have been covered in straw. The fish-catch was brought in here. The children were taught here." David Thomas confirmed this: "This church was the marketplace, the courthouse, the schoolroom. There would have been animals in here. It still *is* the largest enclosed space in Wivenhoe."

Despite its Victorian facade and distinctive 18th century cupola, St. Mary's is actually much older than it might at first appear. The floor plan, David assured me, is from the late 1200s. Before that there was almost certainly an earlier Saxon building. "Wiffa, or whoever the Saxon was who founded Wivenhoe, when he converted to Christianity, would have built a wooden church here, on a site very near the main stockade," he said. Wooden churches, though, tended to burn down quite frequently. People were sometimes careless with candles or fires. When the rather more pragmatic Normans invaded us, they came up with plan B and began using stone for their buildings.

"It would probably have been quite raucous in the old days – when they celebrated the big masses, for instance. Everyone would have been here. People wouldn't have been married in the church itself though. They'd have been married in the porch. But they wanted to be *near* the church for the wedding." This practice, says

David, probably continued right up to the Hardwicke Act of 1753, which put an end to common-law marriage. Before that, the bride's and the groom's fathers would have exchanged dowries, the couple would have jumped the broomstick and been declared married in the porch. He added: "A vicar may or may *not* have been involved." Surprisingly enough, David told me that he now only conducts about twelve weddings a year at St. Mary's. "It used to be more." he said – rather regretfully. He put it down to 'the commercialisation of the wedding industry': "People can afford now to hire a big venue. They have a very short ceremony, then go into the next room and have a reception. I think that for people who have no connection with the Church, it probably makes sense."

When I talked to David on the subject of ghosts, exorcisms and hauntings, he said that although he had occasionally counselled people who had been 'troubled', he himself had never encountered anything of that nature. He had never performed an exorcism, for instance. He said that the Church did have a procedure for such things but that it was a rather specialist area. I replied that I'd learned of a survey a few years earlier that had been conducted among people of all faiths, in order to establish the extent of their spiritual or psychic experiences. Of all the faiths canvassed, the poll concluded, people of the Anglican faith had yielded the fewest experiences. David said that this did not surprise him – although he didn't expand upon the matter.

As for me, in common with many people, I am sometimes aware of increasingly frantic attempts from certain quarters to modernise the Church of England. A gay friend of mine thinks that the Church's chief problem, at the moment, is one of constantly shooting itself in the foot, by bringing sexual politics to the fore. I myself, though, don't care if a bishop happens to be gay or not. But I don't need him to elaborate on the matter. I reason that I also wouldn't care if, say, my accountant or my dustman were gay either. Like most people I just want to know what my Schedule D number is, or when my cans and bottles will be collected.

If I have one big problem with the modern Church, it lies with what is usually referred to as the 'happy-clappy' movement. I might catch an occasional glimpse of this side of Christianity by accidentally tuning into a TV programme such as *Songs of Praise*. For here are the well-scrubbed anodyne faces of modern Christianity, making cringeworthy attempts at 'rocking it up' as they bang tambourines and jiggle clumsily from side to side. The lyrics of Christian rock songs always make God sound a bit like a benevolent Human Resources Officer who occupies the office upstairs in the Civil Service building where we all work together. Is this what the Big Fellow now boils down to in our sterile age – a *nice guy* – a sort of hybrid of Tony Blair and Dale Winton – one who, if you find yourself in confusion, knows all the finer points of filling in Form E125B? This is God as counsellor. All that now remains for you to do is to find your way upstairs to his office and he'll go through things with you over tea and biccies. He may even keep a Fender six-string in the stationery cupboard, which he plunks away at during his lunch break. Who knows? Even as a disinterested party, I'd hate to think so. And as a product of rock-culture myself, I hate the very idea of people twanging electric guitars, banging drum-kits and blasting saxophones in the church while the congregation all yell and shimmy along with it, Gospel style. The Devil may *not* have all the best tunes; it's true. But he tends to make the best rock'n'roll ramalama, so I reckon I'll stick with Lucifer on that front. If, however, I were ever to become a churchgoer, I think I'd probably want something fustily reverential and traditional, replete with all the old descending bass lines and swirling drawbars.

Whenever senior churchmen nowadays *do* get themselves into the headlines, fulminating from the pulpit against this or that modern ill, they frequently seem to do so with the most appalling timing. They, I'm sure, take their cue from the Bible story of Jesus turning over the moneylenders' tables in the temple, with the anger of the righteous. Unfortunately, it doesn't always pan out like that to a skeptical world looking on. The media will routinely make mincemeat out of such ecumenical hissy-fits, pointing out how out of touch clergymen are and ridiculing them still further. It does make you wonder how *in touch* some of the archbishops actually are with their own rank and file.

St. Mary's in Wivenhoe, though, is a good working church possessed of a kindly atmosphere. To an outsider such as myself, this venerable old institution, as it's been run by the 'Rev Dave' at least, seems rather an open and tolerant sort of place – an old-fashioned tailor's shop for the human soul. If you're spiritually inclined that way, the Church is probably a brilliant idea. It ain't broke. They don't need to fix it. And on a spring Sunday, with the blossom from the cherry-plum tree by the railway bridge snowing down over the pavement, the faithful will still walk, smart coated down the High Street in a dazzle of cold sunlight. And in the run-up to Eastertide, the jackdaws will start from the belfry as St. Mary's ham-fisted church bells stutter out their song over the hungover rooftops of the faithless. Long may they continue to do so. I, for one, wish them no ill whatsoever.

Chapter Sixteen

Into The Trees

I have a wonderful old book called *A Handbook To The Environs of London*. It was originally published in 1876 and written by James Thorne, an antiquary and artist. If you look up West Ham, the book will say:

"*West Ham, Essex, a village lying to the E. of Stratford on the road to Plaistow.*"

The Handbook will also tell you that Stratford itself is in Essex. Of Forest Gate, it says:

"*Forest Gate is a hamlet lying to the N. of Upton Road at the edge of Wanstead Flats, the southern extremity of Epping Forest, to which this was the entrance gate. Forest Gate is a station on the Great Eastern railway (main Colchester line). By it, is the Eagle and Child, tea gardens and a holiday resort...*"

Forest Gate, as the book tells you, was the gate to the Great Forest of Essex. This forest once reached north to within about three miles of Colchester. To the east, it extended to the sea and to the west it bordered Hertfordshire. Until Bad King John started hacking large chunks of it down at the beginning of the 13th century – a process referred to as "disafforestation" – Essex was a heavily wooded county.

Forests, though, for many centuries, generally belonged to kings. Naturally, the kings liked hunting in them. If you are a king, you don't want poor commoners and sundry other yobbos taking your royal deer down and eating them before you can get around to doing so yourself. The forests, therefore, were policed by the king's foresters. A forester was a cross between a tree surgeon and a security man and he helped enforce the King's laws, which, if you were a peasant, were punishingly strict. For instance, in certain areas, unless you were a member of the clergy, you weren't allowed to own a dog over a certain size – just in case it could be used for bringing down a deer. If you *did* happen to own a dog over the permitted size, you could still keep it but it had to be lamed first. This was done by the process of cutting out the balls of one of the creature's feet. The operation was usually performed by the foresters and was known as 'laweing'. This is probably how Hounslow, in Middlesex got its name. Hounslow Heath, then within the borders of the Forest of Staines, was the point at which your large hound had to be 'lawed' to prevent him chasing the King's deer. See? Stick with me and you'll learn something new every day.

Although King John, Richard the Lionheart's barking-mad brother, did actually cut down a huge amount of the Great Forest of Essex, other monarchs seem to have been rather better caretakers. Despite this fact, nowadays, what remains of the Great Forest is only a tiny fraction of what it once must have been. Hainault Forest, for instance, took a severe hammering in 1851, losing about 3,000 acres over a six week period of officially sanctioned deforestation. Over the following 150 years, industry, war requirements and rascally developers have depleted the woodland still further.

The result is that now, instead of one great forest, we have several smaller ones, such as Hainault, Hatfield and Epping. A later scourge which afflicted Essex woodland was Dutch Elm Disease, which arrived in the 1960s. Essex lanes and fields were once noted for their beautiful elm trees until, over a few short years, we lost thousands of them to the blight.

The vestiges of the Great Forest of Essex, however, may still be seen in certain places. Brentwood, for instance, as you pass through it by train, is still a heavily wooded area. If, as sometimes happens, your train breaks down between Brentwood and Chelmsford, you may be lucky enough to be stalled in a patch of thick deciduous woodland. On a still autumn afternoon, when the leaves are at their most colourful, being stuck in such a location is infinitely more fun than staring at a stretch of the busy A12 for an hour. It also gives you an idea of what once covered about half of the county and where people went for bank holidays before trains were invented. In the wake of the Industrial Revolution, as the old East End sprawled out, gradually consuming former Essex hamlets and villages such as Stratford and West Ham, the factory workers would take their bank holiday outings in Epping Forest. The railways had not yet reached the coast, and the far-off seaside, in those days, was not a place within range of the average day tripper. The Eastenders in the thousands, therefore, would decamp for picnics and sport to the retreating edges of what had once been the Great Forest of Essex.

Visiting local woodland today can be an interesting experience. A few years ago, Wivenhoe Woods, for instance, suddenly developed a large signboard with a pretty little plastic covered map on it. This was soon vandalised by members of Da Yoof, who drew grafitti on it, stubbed fags out on it, and attempted to burn it with cigarette lighters. The sign informed visitors that our woods had now been rebranded as Ancient Woodland. The latest sign to go up says Wivenhoe Woods Woodland. Much catchier, I reckon. They must have stayed up all night thrashing that one out.

Wivenhoe Woods, on their eastern side, are owned by Wivenhoe Town Council and are largely unmanaged. This first section of woodland is a pleasing tangle of hawthorn and blackthorn and, after strong autumn gales, the ground is strewn with useful bits of kindling for fires. In early spring, when the woods gradually green-up again after winter, the cuckoopint is first up out of the damp ground. Later comes the cow parsley and the young nettles. Finally the blackthorns and the hawthorns blossom and the spring easterlies strew the woodland floor with their petals which, on certain days, can resemble a light fall of snow. In an increasingly transient world, such events are some of the last remaining constants in our lives. I never get bored with observing them.

The western side of the woods is owned by the Borough Council and is managed. Here, where the land rises up to steeper ground overlooking the River Colne, are the tall chestnut trees. They are thought to have been introduced by the Romans who planted chestnut trees all over Europe, chiefly for the use of their wood. The Green family of Wivenhoe have managed and coppiced this part of the woods for many years now. Every few years or so, a swathe of the chestnuts are cut down to allow light to the woodland floor and to prevent the remaining trees from getting too spindly. After winter coppicing, when spring finally arrives, the newly cleared woods can look unexpectedly beautiful. Often the removal of a belt of trees will expose views to the river, open up the woodland canopy and give a different aspect to the topography of the place. Later in the year, when the basal growth springs up from the coppiced tree stumps, it can endow the woodland slopes with a completely new feel. In fact, Adam Green, who manages the woods now, once told me that he often thought that the woods looked at their best when this had occurred. In early May then, when the bluebells and milkmaids come up along the new woodland rides, the visual effect can be breathtaking.

For about fifteen years, when I was still owned by a dog, I was in the woods most days of my life several times a day. When you spend this amount of time there, you get to know the place very well. It's amazing how the woods change from season to season and from year to year. Woodland paths, for instance, may change direction because, say, a tree has fallen in a gale, forcing walkers to alter their route. At other times an old path may disappear altogether and a new one may be created elsewhere, for no reason other than someone decided to go another way and others followed. Quite apart from this, the soil under our woods, which, like much of Wivenhoe, is a mix of stony ballast and London clay, has its own erratic watercourses. Streams will appear in wet weather or, occasionally, dry up in hot summers. Sometimes, like the paths, they too will disappear altogether, only to spring up again after a few years during a period of heavy rainfall. At other times, kids may dam up a particular stream, creating a pool or a marshy patch elsewhere, which will in turn change the route of an old path and create a new one in its place. It's timeless sort of stuff.

Along with all the other meddling of our more recent rulers, there's been a degree of tinkering with the woods too. The officials charged with such things build special little 'heritage walks' or sometimes erect posts with silly looking arrows on them. Such people are terrifically fond of signs and frequently use words like 'heritage' in order to explain their actions. The signs often tell you how valuable the various species of flora and fauna that surround you are. The government experts assume that you might not know or guess that you're in such an environment and will often get volunteers to build special paths for you to walk on, so that you can view things more easily. Such walkways are made with 'sustainable' wooden boards which are 'responsibly sourced'. They are also covered in wire netting, to prevent you from slipping over and suing the council. The same authorities create picnic areas and wheelchair access routes. They just can't stop dicking around with perfectly good bits of English woodland, which had previously done us all fine for years. Until, that is, some desk jockey needed to justify his newly created position as Chief Woodland Wibbling Co-ordinator – or whatever he's called now. The net result of all this tinkering is hard to measure, since there doesn't seem to be any more or any fewer visitors to the woods than there ever were. For instance, I have rarely seen a wheelchair-bound person or even a mobility scooter in the woods, though I daresay that they arrive from time to time. This is a cherishable initiative though and I'm looking forward to the day when we get an official signer appointed, so that deaf people can enjoy the sounds of woodland birdsong too.

Woodlands (with a little bit of judicious coppicing and some occasional making safe by woodmen such as Adam Green, who has known and loved the Wivenhoe woods since he was a child) seem to pretty much run themselves. I preferred the ancient 'heritage woodland' when it was just called 'the woods'. The only provisions needed for such woods were usually a pair of wellies for wet days when they became muddy. Wivenhoe Woods aren't really that big and it's hard to get lost in them. Despite this, I did once come across an entire family who'd managed somehow to do it. Six or seven of them were standing in a patch of thick undergrowth looking concerned as they encouraged their brawny teenage son to beat his way with a stick through some tall nettles for them. I asked them if they were lost.

They looked at me as if I were a member of a strange tribe. I said: " Follow me." In less than a minute I led them onto a path and said, "Stay on that and it'll lead you out. By the way, where are you staying?" They gave me the name of a street bordering the woods at the Wivenhoe Cross end of the town. "Are you visiting?" I asked them. "No. We live here," they told me. I asked them if they'd only just moved into the area. "No," they said. They'd been living here for five years. Since it was a sunny bank holiday and family members were staying, they'd decided to go for a walk in the woods. They'd never done it before. Now they were lost. The teenage boy was only doing his valiant best to help them beat their way to freedom. I hope that they subsequently managed, with the help of counselling, to put the ordeal behind them and to rebuild their shattered lives. I scanned the local papers for weeks afterwards hoping to find something more about the outcome. But there was nothing. Perhaps that's why all those signs have had to go up lately. Maybe the heritage people really *do* know something about modern life which I don't. It's just that I'm reluctant to conclude that we, as a people, are any more stupid than we were forty years ago, though I sometimes fear that it may be the case.

Despite centuries of deforestation, our area is not too badly off for woods. If you get to know one particular patch of woodland well, it's surprising, when you visit another piece of woodland, as to how it may vary in its general feel. Cockayne's Wood, near Alresford, has a completely different sort of atmosphere to Wivenhoe's woods. In late autumn, I've occasionally come across Fly Agaric mushrooms growing at the foot of silver birch trees – a thing that I've never seen in Wivenhoe. Donyland Woods, over the river by Rowhedge, are different again and feel much more like forest. The trees are bigger and older and the echo, which reverberates in them when dogs and kids are running around, makes it feel like an altogether vaster place.

Even in tame and friendly old Wivenhoe Woods, though, you'll occasionally see something surprising – a muntjac deer for instance. Once, several years ago – one scorching hot afternoon in late summer – at the top of the slope, a snake slithered across the path in front of me and disappeared into the undergrowth. It was not a domestic species. I know this because it was about four feet long, black and had bright yellow bands on it. If I didn't know better I'd have said it was a banded krait, a tropical species which I'd seen once or twice when I lived in Malaya. I have no idea what it was doing there and I've never seen such a thing since, but it certainly wasn't one of our own.

The famous Beast of Essex, thought to be a large wild cat, has also been spotted this side of the river. In 2008, this elusive creature was seen by a woman and her daughter as they were driving up Turner Road in Colchester. Only a few months later, a policeman saw what was possibly the same beast mooching around at the back of the Wivenhoe police station in the small hours.

Big cats have become something of a sub-industry in this country, after the Beast of Bodmin – a sort of Elvis among big cats – first made headlines in the 1980s. So many and varied were the sightings that, following several reports of mutilated moorland sheep in 1995, the Ministry of Agriculture lumbered into action and launched an official investigation. On one occasion, Royal Marines were sent out with rifles to see if they could shoot the creature and on another, RAF personnel lay in wait with night-vision devices – all meeting with no success. The investigation's grudging conclusion was that: "...it could not prove that a big cat was *not* present."

News coverage on the subject of big cats tends to be tantalising,if ultimately unsatisfying. Typical eyewitness reports usually describe the creature as being: "About the size of an alsatian – but nothing like a dog in appearance." The accompanying photograph often depicts a cougar or panther similar to the one sighted but, crucially, not the animal itself.

There's probably something in our collective psyche that actually wants there to be a big dangerous cat out roaming the woods and farmland. In the past, though, attempts to create a beast for Essex, which might rival the cachet of the Bodmin animal have been largely unsuccessful. 'The Beast of Brentwood' – a sort of Billy Fury to the Bodmin cat's Elvis – came close, after being sighted in a country park but never quite managed the follow-up hits. Over recent years there have been sightings near Rowhedge, Maldon and Billericay, as well as the one at Turner Road. But somehow, the Turner Road Cat just doesn't carry that authentic ring of terror. *Turner Road Cat Sighted In Garden* wouldn't really convince us, anymore than a beast sighted at say, Lexden or Wivenhoe would. Readers would merely imagine a rather distracted-looking puma in half-moon specs, gazing wistfully into a closed delicatessen window.

If Essex really is aiming to go up in the big cat charts, we need something much more impressive to usurp the Beast of Bodmin's supremacy. Perhaps it could be small group of big cats, lovable and yet slightly dangerous, whom the public could get to know by their individual names – a sort of Beatles of big cats, if you like. An expert might be wheeled out to say that he thought that "groups of big cats were on their way out," and then be proved wrong when the cats in question made an early evening appearance in Colchester's Castle Park, delighting crowds by roaring at bewildered drunks, before running triumphantly off towards the Riverside Estate.

In truth, though, this whole big cats obsession almost certainly began with the Dangerous Wild Animals Act of 1976. The act was brought in because of a growing fashion in the 1960s and 70s for keeping wild animals in private houses. Incredibly, up until the act was passed, in theory at least, it was still possible to keep a panther with a diamanté collar attached to a silver chain in your penthouse. Indeed, if you had the money, one famous London store could even legally obtain you one. What better present for a pop star's high maintenance American girlfriend than an adorable lynx? Or for the exiled foreign tyrant, biding his time in England until he could return to his own country again, how about a cheerful pair of tiger cubs for the walled compound? All manner of exotic and dangerous creatures were alleged to be living in private homes before the act went through Parliament. As a result, many creatures were released into the wild after its implementation. This has been the probable cause of sightings ever since.

You can understand how it might have happened. That panther cub that you bought on impulse some months back is now a fully-grown and, frankly, unco-operative adolescent that doesn't quite fit into the weekend cottage at Elmstead Market. It's destroyed the Chesterfield and regularly overpowers your terrified dog. It's the cause of marital disharmony, huge veterinary and cleaning bills and is also, now, illegal. What do you do? Answer: you feed it three crushed up valium, stick it in the boot of the hatchback, drive it to Great Bentley Green at dead of night and watch it stagger out of your life. Job jobbed. Months later it meets the former Beast of Brentwood in a spinney near West Bergholt and they get on famously. The Essex countryside subsequently becomes a kind of slow-food restaurant and dating mecca for big cats. Thirty years on and we have a situation.

After the Wivenhoe big cat sighting, I wrote the following entry in my web diary.

It's been seen again. This time in small hours of Tuesday night. A large puma described his shock at seeing a policeman in Wivenhoe. "I was just round the back of the police station mooching around, when I heard what I thought was a car engine. Upon coming round the side of the building to investigate, there he was, lit up in my night vision. He had a sort of dark coat, a peaked cap and must have stood round about six foot tall. I think he was probably as surprised to see me as I was to see him. I mean, you used to get stories, back in the 1970s and 1980s, about policemen prowling around – especially in the area of the police station. But in recent years, with sightings becoming less frequent, I'd more or less put it all down to local legend – people who'd had a bit too much to drink and that sort of thing. I would say that the creature that I saw, if it was a policeman, was fully grown. It may have been a parking warden of course; they're rather more common in Wivenhoe now and easily mistaken for policemen in the dark. I can pretty much discount that though, because parking wardens are nearly all diurnal and have a different sort of gait. If the creature I saw was a policeman, then it brings all sorts of safety issues into question. Policemen won't usually harm you however. Not unless something alarms him like, say, a recent terrorist scare. During times like this, if he's armed, he might just start shooting at you. More commonly, he'll probably just be getting on with whatever it is that policemen do – filling in forms, post coding bicycles and so on. One old lady, who lives locally, even claimed that the creatures could be approached with cups of tea and biscuits, provided that you do it very gently of course. I must warn feral cats though: If you do see a policeman, don't panic, he'll probably just walk the other way. Recent reports that 100 new policemen have been released into the wild are still speculative. However, you're far more likely to see a policeman in the town than in a village, so the public shouldn't worry unduly at this stage.

Away from the woods themselves, there are plenty of trees around Wivenhoe and one of my favourites, a huge horse chestnut, stands just outside the police station. In April, the leaves suddenly unfurl in luminescent green and within a short month, the whole tree will be adorned in pink-crowned creamy looking 'candles'. It's ironic, however, that what most people think of as being a particularly English tree is actually an import from the Balkans – one that didn't make its way here until the 17th century. Despite a resemblance both in foliage and fruit to the sweet chestnut tree, it's an entirely unrelated species.

I was always told by my mum that the burnished brown conkers the tree produces were poisonous. This was partially proved one autumn during my childhood, when I brought a bag of them into the house and the Jack Russell swallowed three before anyone could stop it. The dog subsequently spent three days ejecting the toxin all over the carpets from various outlets and, despite its complete recovery, my cursing mother banned conkers from the house ever afterwards.

The Turks, though, used to give conkers to their horses to sort out digestive problems, so the nuts aren't poisonous to all animals. Quite the opposite, in fact. During the Great War it was discovered that a flour useful for animal fodder could be processed from conkers, a ton of which, during shortages, would make enough meal to free up quantities of conventional flour for human consumption. The manufacturers found that cattle and sheep would eat the meal quite happily, though pigs, for some reason, wouldn't touch it.

Yet it's only in England, so far as I know, that small boys play the game of 'conkers', where the nuts are bored through with a skewer, strung on string and then smashed to smithereens. Whenever I've asked them, neither German nor French children seem to be familiar with the practice. In Essex though, in early September, before the conkers are quite ready, you'll see gangs of boys hurling sticks up into trees in their clumsy attempts to get the immature nuts to fall. They fall in their own good time of course and always will do but the resonance of the childhood game sometimes persists into adulthood. Several times, I have witnessed homegoing commuters, grown men, pick up a handful from the path and put them in their pockets. The conkers, of course, often end up on sideboards, kitchen tables or even office desks. There exists a residual affection for them because they evoke lost childhood, autumns past and old games. And from Forest Gate, where the Great Forest of Essex once began, all the way up the line to Wivenhoe, as the nights draw in, the conkers fall, spilling from their spiky husks to lie gleaming on the paths and in the gutters. They mark the passing of the year. They are treasures from the edge of the woods.

Lightning Source UK Ltd.
Milton Keynes UK
27 March 2010

152006UK00001B/9/P